Cambridge Elements ☰

Elements in Environmental Humanities
edited by
Louise Westling
University of Oregon
Serenella Iovino
University of North Carolina at Chapel Hill
Timo Maran
University of Tartu

ITALO CALVINO'S ANIMALS

Anthropocene Stories

Serenella Iovino
University of North Carolina at Chapel Hill

CAMBRIDGE
UNIVERSITY PRESS

University Printing House, Cambridge CB2 8BS, United Kingdom

One Liberty Plaza, 20th Floor, New York, NY 10006, USA

477 Williamstown Road, Port Melbourne, VIC 3207, Australia

314–321, 3rd Floor, Plot 3, Splendor Forum, Jasola District Centre,
New Delhi – 110025, India

103 Penang Road, #05–06/07, Visioncrest Commercial, Singapore 238467

Cambridge University Press is part of the University of Cambridge.

It furthers the University's mission by disseminating knowledge in the pursuit of
education, learning, and research at the highest international levels of excellence.

www.cambridge.org
Information on this title: www.cambridge.org/9781009065306
DOI: 10.1017/9781009063586

First published 2021

A catalogue record for this publication is available from the British Library.

ISBN 978-1-009-06530-6 Paperback
ISSN 2632-3125 (online)
ISSN 2632-3117 (print)

Italo Calvino's Animals

Anthropocene Stories

Elements in Environmental Humanities

DOI: 10.1017/9781009063586
First published online: August 2021

Serenella Iovino
University of North Carolina at Chapel Hill

Author for correspondence: Serenella Iovino, serenella.iovino@unc.edu

Abstract: The words "Anthropocene animals" conjure pictures of dead albatrosses' bodies filled with plastic fragments, polar bears adrift on melting ice sheets, solitary elephants in the savannah. Suspended between the impersonal nature of the Great Extinction and the singularity of exotic individuals, these creatures appear remote, disconnected from us. But animals in the Anthropocene are not simply "out there." Threatening and threatened, they populate cities and countryside, often trapped in industrial farms, zoos, labs. Among them, there are humans, too. *Italo Calvino's Animals* explores Anthropocene animals through the visionary eyes of a classic modern author. In Calvino's stories, ants, cats, chickens, rabbits, gorillas, and other critters emerge as complex subjects and inhabitants of a world under siege. Beside them, another figure appears in the mirror: that of an *anthropos* without a capital *A*, the epitome of subaltern humans with their challenges and inequalities, a companion species on the difficult path of coevolution.

Keywords: Italo Calvino, animals, Italian literature, anthropocene, ecocriticism

ISBNs: 9781009065306 (PB), 9781009063586 (OC)
ISSNs: 2632-3125 (online), 2632-3117 (print)

Contents

1 Introduction

On November 17, 1946, Italo Calvino, then a 23-year-old journalist and would-be writer, published a curious article in *L'Unità*, the Italian Communist Party's newspaper with which he collaborated. Titled "Goats are Watching Us," the article reported on a commemoration of the "goats sacrificed for humanity's sake" organized by the farmers of San Fernando Valley, California. Some will observe, he wrote, that no similar ceremony has ever been held for the children, women, and old people killed by bombs in Hiroshima, Turin, or Milan, who died without knowing why "on the altar of war's needs." In the goats' commemoration, however, Calvino saw "a secret remorse of humankind towards animals, united to a typically human hypocrisy." He added:

> Have you ever asked yourselves what the goats on Bikini must have thought? And the cats in bombed houses? And the dogs in war zones? And the fish struck by torpedoes? How must they have judged us humans in those moments, in their logic – which exists and, although simpler, is . . . a much more humane logic?
>
> Yes, we do owe animals an explanation, if not a reparation. . . . We must apologize to them if we upset this world which is also theirs, if we involve them in business that does not concern them. (Calvino 2001: II, 2131–2132. My translation)

The inspiring reason for the article and these peculiar considerations is a remarkable event that was well in line with the climate of the period. That same year, in July, the United States had conducted the so-called Operation Crossroads, detonating a couple of atomic bombs at the Bikini Atoll, and some goats had been "sacrificed" in the experiment. This piece contains, therefore, a significant historical find, apart from the pulverized caprines: the radiation of nuclear fallout. According to geologists, this very fallout – and that of the bombs that, before and after, were tested by the thousands on both sides of the Iron Curtain – might mark the "Golden Spike," namely the ground zero, of a new period which would affect all life on Earth: the Anthropocene.

This novel "Age of the Human," which would definitively close the brief Holocene adventure, has been a subject of debate for some years now. Geologists talk about it, although the International Stratigraphy Commission has not yet officially ratified its entry into geology textbooks.[1] Even more,

---

[1] The first official proposal to call "Anthropocene" the last phase of the Quaternary is by Paul Crutzen and Eugene Stoermer (2000). As of May 2021, the hypothesis is still being evaluated by the International Commission on Stratigraphy (ICS) and the International Union of Geological Sciences (IUGS). However, on August 29, 2016, the ICS Anthropocene Working Group (AWG) presented a formal recommendation oriented toward recognition at the International Geological Congress. In May 2019, the AWG voted in favor of submitting a formal proposal to the ICS by

humanists talk about it, especially those who are interested in environmental issues. This is not surprising. The constitution of this period does indeed have a powerful narrative force: for the first time, a geological model manages to accommodate within a single frame apparently disconnected phenomena, such as climate change due to the modification of atmospheric chemistry, the upheaval of the surface and depths of our planet, mass extinctions, ecosystem pollution, social injustices, and (unsurprisingly) global pandemics.

Speaking of narrative force is not hyperbole. It is also thanks to the Anthropocene *as a framework* that the interweaving of these phenomena is revealed, which we now see not only as interdependent but also as linked to a common trigger: the profound and pervasive impact of our species. For those who observe it with the eyes of history or literature, then, the Anthropocene no longer seems just a hypothesis of geologists, but the plot of a huge planetary novel.

A few years ago, while studying Calvino, an Italian author who happens to be one of the foremost novelists of the twentieth century, I noticed a series of curious coincidences. Starting at the end of World War II, the parable of his works ran parallel to the major phases of the Great Acceleration: the upsurging growth rate that signals the impact of human activity on the planet's cycles, and hence the beginning of the Anthropocene. Not only that: writing about nuclear fallout and the changing atmosphere and climate, the avalanche of concrete that would bury age-old landscapes, the inequalities propagating across industrial society, and the ways life forms were being affected by all these changes, Calvino was following, step by step, what we now recognize as the progression of this epoch, its manifold strata. In fact, even if the geological notion was only to arise half a century later, the effects of modernity on atmosphere, lithosphere, biosphere, and sociosphere were already perfectly visible in the Italy of his time. And they were emerging simultaneously in his novels and stories, which might be read as a "narrative stratigraphy" of this new epoch.[2]

In my explorations, the sphere of life came to occupy a prominent space. In particular, I found it fascinating and insightful how Calvino represented animals by putting them in constant conversation with the world and time to which they belong. Whether parts of an evolving rural ecology or trapped in the cages of a zoo, helpless victims of science or residues of wildness in a city that swallows every critter free and untamed, these animals appeared to me as epitomes of the

---

2021, situating the Golden Spike around the mid-twentieth century (beginning of the atomic era). Data available at: http://quaternary.stratigraphy.org/working-groups/anthropocene/.

[2] For a reconstruction of this "narrative stratigraphy" through a literary-textual reading of Calvino's works, see Iovino 2018. On the Anthropocene's "extraordinary strata" (lithosphere, atmosphere, biosphere, and sociosphere), see Zalasiewicz 2016.

Anthropocene life. So, I decided to delve into this fictional (and yet so real) biosphere by selecting from Calvino's literary animals those representing the forms of global displacement, alienation, alteration, and extinction that characterize nonhuman (and human) existence in our days.

Global displacement, alienation, alteration, and extinction: these categories are not listed at random. In fact, the current state of life forms on planet Earth is terribly complicated and deserves a few preliminary considerations before we start our investigation of Calvino's stories. As one authoritative study put it, the Anthropocene biosphere possesses

> four key parameters: (1) the widespread (near-global) resetting of ecosystem composition and structure, partly as a result of cross-global species invasions; (2) a major change in the energy budget that all species rely upon . . . with one species (*Homo sapiens*) consuming some 25% to 40% of net primary production . . .; (3) the human-directed evolution of plants and animals; and (4) the increasing coupling of the biosphere with an ever more rapidly evolving technosphere. (Williams et al. 2015: 5)

Let's summarize: invasion of alien species, human overexploitation of the planet's resources, systematic disruption of ecosystems and habitats, and technological manipulation of life. Taken singularly, these phenomena are already enough to dramatically alter the conditions of living beings and ecosystems. Combined, they trigger an amplified array of cascade effects, of which the most staggering and macroscopic one is what biologists call the Sixth Extinction: the biggest die-off of life forms since the Cretaceous–Tertiary (K–T) extinction event, nearly 66 million years ago, when three-quarters of the plant and animal species on Earth were wiped out by a comet or asteroid.

Not by chance, the American anthropologist Anna Tsing and her research collective in Aarhus, Denmark, describe the Anthropocene as a landscape populated by "ghosts" and "monsters" (Tsing et al. 2017). Ghosts are the shadows cast by extinction: they emerge from the multitude of absences left behind by this quiet systemic loss that obliterates "living arrangements that took millions of years to put into place" (Gan et al. 2017: G1). Monsters are the presences filling these empty hollows: hybrid and invasive species, parasites, creatures whose genes have been damaged by radioactivity and pollution, and all the forces at work in the hazy zones of an altered biology (including, of course, viruses). In these landscapes, "urban" and "rural" become blurred categories, both being permeable terrains for larger-scale dynamics. Infiltrated by the erratic effects of global exchanges, for example, the country often becomes a setting for dark pastoral: a planetary plantation where cultures are homogenized and new slaveries established, or a conquest territory for alien organisms that travel with goods along the borderless routes of world commerce. On the other hand, cities, with their rarefying "green" spots, turn into accidental habitats for feral species or temporary shelters for marginal creatures and people. And, where "nature" is no longer at home in urban areas, these very cities also become spaces of confinement or coerced domestication, where the cultural and the technological merge with the biological in problematic ways. This happens in labs, zoos, industrial farms, and all the places where our bioschizophrenic modernity situates those beings that are considered disposable – or just, irreducibly, "others." Life in the Anthropocene, in other words, is often an "alter-life": a life which has been altered and "othered" by human intervention.

All this raises issues of justice both within and among species. Social justice, too, is one of the matters at stake in the Anthropocene biosphere. This is why some theorists prefer names such as "Capitalocene" or "Plantationocene," stressing the fact that the real culprit is not a generic "human being," but the political and economic systems involved in the commodification of natural forms: capitalism, imperialism, colonialism, neoliberalism, and new slaveries.[3] Like the dying and vilified nonhuman others, the subaltern, colonized, marginalized humans are also victims of an *Anthropos* with which they certainly do not identify. The human experience of social injustice is also part of the larger picture of our biosphere. And, finally, the Anthropocene affects species in all their environments: environments of life and of meanings. Its dynamics shake individuals with their fragile balances, their challenges and inequalities, their signs, their stories.

All these themes and articulations of the Anthropocene life are present in Calvino's work, and this Element will heed some of them. A real case of alien species invasion, for example, is the subject of *The Argentine Ant* (published in 1952), where the composition of the Riviera's biota, transformed by little arthropods accidentally imported from the Paraná region, distorts the physiognomy of a landscape, turning a familiar place into a dissonant and uncanny dimension (Section 2). The clash between the "city of men" and the habitat of feral species, within an urban space that is "full of refugees . . . without refuge,"

---

[3] "Capitalocene" is the name popularized by Jason Moore (2015, 2016a), and elaborated by him, Andreas Malm, and Donna Haraway. "Plantationocene" is a coinage by Anna Tsing (2015). Haraway (2016) adds to these terms the positive "Chthulucene," which is, more than an existing age, a project meant to overcome bad "-cenes" in the name of multispecies companionships. Historian Charles Mann (2011) has proposed the name "Homogenocene," meaning the global homogenization of ecosystem composition and cultures developing from the imperialist expansion inaugurated by Columbus's travels. More recently, Marco Armiero (2021) has proposed the term "Wasteocene," through which, stressing the omnipresence of waste in the earth's bio-geophysical cycles, he also pinpoints the mechanisms of exclusion that underlie the production of waste at the material, social, and political levels.

as Donna Haraway says (2016: 160), is one of the leitmotivs of *Marcovaldo*, and in particular of the episode "The Garden of Stubborn Cats," which is at the same time an elegy for Holocene coexistences and a hymn to resilient hybrid communities (Section 3). And, prominently, Calvino writes about the dark zones where the Anthropocene confines and "others" its living bodies: the lab, the factory, and the zoo, which are par excellence the places where humans subjugate other beings, generating forms of domination that delve into their very flesh. In these three sites – whose appearance on a mass scale coincides with the beginning of the industrial era – the fate of animals frequently converges with that of disempowered people, as we will see in the stories of "The Poisonous Rabbit" (Section 4), "The Workshop Hen" (Section 5), and "The Albino Gorilla" (Section 6). Finally, Calvino also tells us something about extinction, which, although not the explicit focus of these stories, casts its shadow on and emerges from them in unexpected forms. The environmental humanities' theoretical toolbox, with research in multispecies ethnography, biosemiotics, animal studies, environmental justice, new materialisms, and posthumanism, will guide us through these texts and themes.

But what makes Italo Calvino (1923–1985) so interesting for a study like this? What can he say to those who look for ecological topics in literature? The answer is easy: everything. His novels and short stories are animated by a basic premise: the need to broaden the gaze of literature beyond the human, focusing on life, on *bios* – and on the imagination that animates this life.

Calvino has been exploring this territory from the very beginning of his career. A son of botanists, he grows up amid an "experimental" garden, where animals and plants populate a landscape that is at the same time tangible and theoretical. At Villa Meridiana, his home but also a research ecosystem in the Western Riviera, mud, insects, birds, and roots cohabit with scientific concepts, Linnean taxonomies, and observation instruments. Into this landscape, Italo brings his passion for political action (he is only twenty-one when he becomes a partisan during the Nazi-Fascist occupation) and his curiosity for everything that makes a story, especially if this story belongs to the world "outside the self." He is an attentive observer and interpreter of the nonhuman, of the reality bubbling beyond our understanding and control. As a mature writer, this sensibility joins his creativity even more powerfully, giving life to strange figures that complement and demystify the imagination of traditional humanism. All this, without giving up a compassionate interest for the human, especially if different, heterodox, or marginalized.

And so, if in *Cosmicomics* (1965) a cartoon-like and paradoxical irony is employed to show the universal kinship of all existing forms, in *Marcovaldo* (1963) a subproletarian *bon sauvage* tries to disentangle the "nature vs. city" jumble as he is called to face precarious housing, poor health, lack of green areas, industrial pollution, and animal welfare. *The Baron in the Trees* (1957) tells the story of the subversive rejection of an ancien-régime dinner which ends up in a life detached from the ground and suspended in the leafy highways of Europe – a story caught just a moment before this wooden world disappears. *The Watcher* (1963) looks for the human in "the last city of imperfection" of disabled men and women. *Invisible Cities* (1972) discloses the endless metamorphoses of urban organisms, dreamed or lived, prefiguring today's debate on life in the age of super-megalopolises and disappearing places. Finally, *Mr. Palomar* (1983) creates, via the eyes of a pensive and irritable middle-aged man, an observatory through which the world can look at itself in all the multifaceted presences outside and around the human.

These are only a few examples of a creativity "beyond the human," that in the course of a short lifetime bloomed into a huge number of stories, novels, essays, articles, poems, opera librettos … And, of course, this Element will not even come close to exhausting the topic of life in Calvino, or that of the animal – a question that "goes to the heart of his project as a writer and an intellectual."[4]

But the goal of any research – whatever its subject or kind – is not to extinguish a topic, but rather to open more discourses, and perhaps elicit new curiosities and questions. A small attempt at stirring up these curiosities and questions, and a modest exercise in the practice of the environmental humanities, this Element is meant to invite its readers along a double path: one that, starting from Calvino's literary animals, ushers in a deeper understanding of the dynamics of life in the Anthropocene, and another that, starting from the Anthropocene animals, ushers in the discovery of one of the protagonists of the twentieth-century literary scene. A double treat, indeed, because both – animated by an imagination which is multiple and singular, alien and intimate, brotherly and surreal – deserve our attention.

Italo Calvino's Life: A Lightning-fast Overview

Italo Calvino was born in Cuba in October 1923 to a couple of Italian scientists. He is two years old when the family moves to Sanremo, in the Liguria region, where an Experimental Floriculture Station will be housed in the family residence, Villa Meridiana, directed by his father, Mario, with the support of his mother, Eva Mameli. Nature is always at home in his imagination, even if as

---

[4] Bolongaro 2009: 107. I borrow the expression "beyond the human" from Past 2019. Elena Past, with Deborah Amberson, is a pioneering figure in animal–humanities-oriented Italian studies. See Amberson and Past 2014. This Element is part of a more comprehensive research-in-progress on Calvino and ecology. That forthcoming work will contain more detailed analyses of issues, texts, and literary examples, that, due to its limited size, could not be included here.

a typically rebellious child he refuses to learn the "technical" language of botany and agronomy, specialties of his parents. In fact, he is the only literary person in a family of scientists: two uncles and their wives are chemists. His younger brother, Floriano, will become a geologist.

Italo is seventeen when Italy enters the war and is not yet twenty-one when the Nazi-Fascist occupation forces him to join the partisan brigades in the Ligurian Alps, going into hiding. He begins to write shortly after, and his stories are stories of places and animals, of soldiers and shyness, of gardens and children, of cities, of eccentric and marginal humans, of rough and mysterious youth mixed with violence and landscape.

After the war he moves to Turin, one of Italy's major industrial cities, then in full postwar reconstruction. There he graduates in literature with a thesis on Joseph Conrad, becomes a journalist, and begins working for the progressive publisher Einaudi, where he remains until 1961. He would later become Einaudi's editorial consultant. An active member of the Italian Communist Party, he moves away from it in 1957, disappointed by the repressive intervention of the USSR in Hungary in 1956. In 1964 he marries Esther "Chichita" Singer, an Argentine translator for UNESCO, in Cuba. The couple, who had met in Paris in 1962, moves to Rome first, where Giovanna is born in 1965, and then back to Paris, where Italo works in close contact with the leading figures of the cultural scene. He is among the animators of OuLiPo (*Ouvroir de Littérature Potentielle*, Workshop of Potential Literature), one of the most original experimental literary groups of the time. Other members are Raymond Queneau, Georges Perec, François Le Lionnais: all people who, like him, enjoy seeing the *ars combinatoria* hidden in stories and words.

Meanwhile, he writes, and in 1980 he returns to Rome, which he will periodically leave for trips abroad and holidays in Tuscany, where the family has a house in the Roccamare pine forest, near Castiglione della Pescaia.

In 1984 he is invited to Harvard to give the prestigious Norton Lectures during the 1985/86 academic year. By the summer of 1985 he has written five out of six of these lectures, and is ready to leave for Massachusetts, when a stroke hits him in September. Less than two weeks later, he dies, aged sixty-one. An absolute protagonist of the modern literary scene, he is one of the most celebrated novelists and intellectuals world-wide.

2 Ants

The landscapes of the Anthropocene are not necessarily gloomy postapocalyptic territories. Some of them, indeed, still possess a certain aesthetic appeal: a beauty, sometimes; and always a vitality, however troublesome and baffling.

Think of Sanremo, today. I agree: it is not that easy to come to terms with the cascade of buildings playing "piggyback with one another" and the thousands of closed windows waiting to be opened by "the Milanese families who [want] a place by the sea" (Calvino 1971: 163–164). However, if viewed from above, the postcard effect is anything but unpleasant. This picture embraces a harbor filled with yachts and cruise ships, the brownish roofs of yellow and pink houses, tiny gardens with plumbago plants, palm trees, and maritime pines timidly punctuating the promenade, with its residual testimonies of Belle Époque splendors. All around, a vast expanse of new houses, almost uninterrupted, mingles with the ancient walls of La Pigna, this dark pinecone shut in its urban scales. Finally, interspersed with small agricultural patches, a huge blanket of greenhouses and geometrically enclosed fields nests one of Europe's biggest industrial flower crops. This is the "inexhaustible surface" that one – a bird, a human, or a drone – sees, flying over Sanremo and its surroundings. But if, for once, one could "venture to seek what's underneath," another landscape would appear. And this is where the Anthropocene grounds become haunted – and haunting.[5] In the pullulating life of the dark soil, the silence of the fields is troubled by "thousands of underground nests," with ants coming and going in "a long procession" (Calvino 1971: 150–151). It is the edge of the Mediterranean megacolony of *Linepithema humile*, the formidable Argentine ant, one of "the world's one hundred worst animal invaders" (Lowe et al.: 2000). Believe it or not, these neverending subterranean labyrinths extend over nearly 4,000 miles (6,000 kilometers), from the coasts of the Italian Riviera to the Atlantic shores of Spain.

Species such as the Argentine ant are very good ambassadors for the biosphere of the Anthropocene. As noted, one of the features of life in this epoch is the extensive resetting of ecosystemic structures due to "cross-global species invasions" (Williams et al. 2015: 5). Of course, these "bioinvaders" do not travel on their own. Whether driven by market, science, or imperialistic expansion, human traffic sometimes causes a deliberate or accidental introduction of species, which are allowed to "cross a natural barrier dispersal," dramatically interfering with the composition of ecosystems. This is not a problem per se, but might become one if an "exotic species," unable to integrate with the "ecological community," damages or degrades "the local ecosystem, displacing or eliminating native species."[6] In the case of *Linepithema humile*, global barrier crossing has been very successful. Native to the Paraná region, this arthropod

---

[5] These quotes and passages allude to *Mr. Palomar*'s famous episode "From the Terrace" (Calvino 1985: 55): "This is how birds think, or at least this is how Mr. Palomar thinks, imagining himself a bird. It is only after you have come to know the surface of things, he concludes, that you can venture to seek what is underneath. But the surface of things is inexhaustible."

[6] Noss and Corripeders 1994: 11–12. On "bioinvaders," see Johnson 2010.

has made its way around the continents, expanding its realms to California, Japan, Hawaii, South Africa, Australia, and even New Zealand.[7]

Italy showed the first signs of ant colonization around the 1920s. From the vantage point of his family's botanic observatory, the young Calvino had firsthand experience of a landscape dominated by industry and flowers, and it is there, in the form of a minuscule but unstoppable nonhuman agent, that the traces of the Anthropocene begin to emerge. We can follow this transformation in *The Argentine Ant*, a novella Italo started writing in 1949 and published in 1952. Due to the almost Kafkaesque character of the story, for many years Calvino had a hard time convincing his readers of its historical accuracy. In a letter he wrote to literary critic Goffredo Fofi on January 30, 1984, he was very clear: "*The Argentine Ant* . . . is the most realistic story I have written in my life; it describes with absolute exactness the situation that came about because of the invasion of the Argentine ants into the cultivated areas of San Remo and a large swathe of the Western Riviera di Ponente during my childhood, in the twenties and thirties."[8] He had been even more explicit thirty years earlier in responding to Cesare Cases, who had interpreted *The Argentine Ant* as an allegory of capitalism:

> Whoever has been in the Riviera knows that there is no exaggeration in my story: facts, characters, struggling methods, different behaviors toward the ants, an ant-dominated life, are constantly part of my childhood experience. (Now, after the adoption of DDT, the situation has slightly changed, but not that much). It is a realistic account, then: one that suggests a definition of *nature* and of the human attitude towards it. . . . I am interested above all in the way nature is considered, which is much more important than all capitalisms and transient epiphenomena; but nature in our eyes is like history – we find in it the same monstrous cruelty of the world in which we live.[9]

A realistic account, a direct personal experience, and an attempt to define "nature" and human attitudes toward it: this was *The Argentine Ant* according to its author. In these statements, the words "monstrous cruelty" are those that strike me the most. Nota bene: not because "nature" is cruel, but because it is *as cruel as* "the world in which we live." However apparently uninterested in following the ripples of capitalism, Calvino was well aware that a monstrous nature was one with the monsters of Capital. Strictly connected to the prosperity of the Riviera, itself a result of the global import-export of plants and the

---

[7] Van Wilgenburg et al. 2010; Inglis-Arkell 2015.

[8] Calvino 2013: 529. In this letter Calvino was commenting on an article by Mario Barenghi, who had defined the novella as "oneiric-Kafkaesque."

[9] December 20, 1958. Calvino 2000: 575. My translation.

industrial transformation of floriculture, the arrival of *Linepithema humile* (formerly classified as *Iridomyrmex humilis*) was indeed one of these monsters.

The ant invasion was particularly problematic in this area, where a Consorzio obbligatorio di difesa contro la formica argentina (Obligatory consortium of protection against the Argentine ant) had been active since the early 1920s.[10] That was also the time when Mario Calvino, a Professor of Agriculture and a small plantation manager, was living across continents. His activities were split among Italy, Mexico, Cuba, and Brazil.[11] Whether the plant specimens he sent to Sanremo from overseas (avocado, grapefruit, and several flower varieties) might have contributed to further entangling the knots of the Anthropocene biosphere is something we will never know for sure. But Italo would not overcome this doubt. According to Domenico Scarpa and Silvio Perrella, the detail that Calvino "mercifully omits" when he insists on the truthfulness of *The Argentine Ant* is that his father might have been unintentionally responsible for the importation of these upsetting aliens: "the ants arrived in the Riviera along with the exotic plants that Mario Calvino had brought with him as he moved back to Italy" from Cuba, where he was working and where Italo was born (Scarpa 1999: 128; Perrella 2010: 45). If proven true, this would be sadly ironic for a man, an agriculturalist, who had invested so much of his energy in innovating the Riviera's plantation systems in a way that would preserve botanical variety and what we now call "biodiversity." As we learn from Calvino's openly autobiographical *The Road to San Giovanni* (1962), his father was fiercely opposed to floral monocultures. However, he could not help feeling guilty vis-à-vis the widespread carnation farms "stretching around in squalid and ferocious geometry" that his work had involuntarily prompted.[12]

Whether or not Mario Calvino played a part in it, by the beginning of the 1920s the ants' invasion was a full-blown case. In 1923, the City Council of Sanremo issued a public alarm, providing a precise delimitation of the infested territory, "where surveillance is mandatory by law, due to the risk that the Riviera's flowers and plants destined to be shipped throughout Italy might become a vehicle of expansion" (Castello, n.d.). And, indeed, this propagation all over Italy was a reality.[13] This gives a sense of how tangible the presence of

---

[10] Its institution was enforced through a decree published in the Gazzetta Ufficiale del Regno d'Italia on July 24, 1922.

[11] See Mez 1974.

[12] Calvino 1993: 31. He also writes that Mario "realized that this thing he had hoped and worked for did mean economic and technical progress for our backward agriculture, yes, but also destruction of wholeness and harmony, loss of variety, subordination to money" (32).

[13] A Decree of the Ministry of Agriculture had declared the ant as "a plague and harmful parasite" as early as 1919: Decreto del Ministero dell'Agricoltura, September 28, 1919, published in

Linepithema humile was during Calvino's youth, and of how profoundly this unsettling agent was affecting his own biosphere. Further confirming the historical truthfulness of the story is the fact that its characters and background, even if unnamed and unspecified, are inspired by the real case of Coldirodi, a small village attached to Sanremo, which specialized in the cultivation of carnations and roses, and where a prosperous colony of immigrants from Abruzzo had settled.[14]

The plot of *The Argentine Ant* is very simple and represents a typical story of internal migration: in their search for better living conditions, a working-class couple and their baby boy move to a small town on the Riviera di Ponente. What they find instead is a massive ant invasion, which makes their everyday life simply impossible, shattering their dream of social improvement.

Through the worried voice of the anonymous protagonist, the story develops into a crescendo of anxiety, rapidly climaxing from the abrupt discovery of the tiny black spots to the sense of total powerlessness and frustration they inspire. The mysterious presence of the ants ("they ... might originate anywhere"; Calvino 1971: 189), almost imperceptible at the beginning, finally becomes overwhelming. The narrative peak reveals the growing disproportion between the insects' uncontainable power and the astonishment of these flustered people, suddenly at the mercy of an inhuman superorganism, "an enemy like fog or sand, against which force [is] useless" (151). The apparently familiar environment thus discloses a dark side made of "thousands of underground nests," feeding on "the thick sticky soil and the low vegetation," plant juices, and decaying animal remains (150). As in all ectopic narratives, what seemed firm and predictable is exposed and vulnerable: "Our new home, although it looked so smooth and solid on the surface, was in fact porous and honeycombed with cracks and holes" (Calvino 1971: 150), we read in a passage. It is clear here that "home" is also "oikos" – at once the individual sphere of domestic intimacy and the larger ecosystemic household of the place, each altered by the eerie combination of global traffic and natural dynamics. With their unnerving and unstoppable frenzy, the ants bring their Argentinian wilderness to literally every corner of this Ligurian home: wardrobe, pantry, even the baby's cradle and his milk bottle (193). After a short while, the house becomes fully "informicata" ("ant-infested") (193). When an ant enters the baby's ear, the infiltration is complete.

Gazzetta Ufficiale, October 8, 1919. In the Gazzetta Ufficiale of July 1922, another Decree of the Ministry for Agriculture (May 27, 1922) prescribed the compulsory destruction of the ant in all territories infested with it.

[14] See Ferrua 1977: 376–377.

This last episode is critically revelatory. What is at stake here is not simply the exposure of a little human to the paradoxical force of these insects, minuscule and yet uncontainable, but rather the incorporation, in the baby's fragile figure, of all the networks of substances and exchanges that are behind the ants' presence in this modest abode. What converges in this body are the commercial routes, the trade of goods, the transnational market agreements, fossil fuel and big ship manufacture, human and animal labor exploited in plantations thousands of miles and hundreds of years away, and the evolutionary history of a species that would never, on its own legs, have crossed the Ocean all the way from the Paraná. All these elements trace back to the impersonal forces that make the Anthropocene. At once, these forces enter the household, penetrating the baby's body. Tiny and defenseless, this body is contrasted with "the Argentine *ant*" (189), a single yet compound individual, similar to what Timothy Morton would define as a hyperobject, an entity that is "massively distributed in time and space relative to humans" (2013: 1). Yet, however infinitely dissimilar they might be, both the small human body and the alien superorganism absorb in themselves the predicaments of this epoch. They are two extremities of the Anthropocene collective.

Between these two extremities, other agents are at work in these corporeal crossings: chemicals. Grotesque side-characters recommend all sorts of improbable poisons, whose names sound like a blend of mythology and hexing rituals: "Profosfàn," "Mirminèc," "Arsopàn," "Arfanàx," etc. The epopee of chemical solutions, however, fails against the "persistent, imperceptible enemy which had taken over our home" (Calvino 1971: 192). The struggle against the ants soon becomes a war, with a battlefield, trenches, and unconventional remedies that are in all respect chemical weapons. And here another chapter opens. With his typical surreal irony, Calvino suggests that the real goal of the "Consortium for Protection against the Argentine Ant" is not to solve the problem, but rather to make it last, implying that there might be bigger financial interests in using these chemicals. The symbol of this speculation is a weird employee who enters uninvited into village houses, spreading every corner with completely useless poisons. Black-dressed and tiny-handed, the "Ant man" is himself an uncanny personification of this alien reality invading the people's households.

As Calvino noted in his 1958 letter to Cesare Cases, the ant invasion might be partially managed with the advent of DDT, which had been employed in Italy since 1945 to eradicate malaria. However, as the existence (and the thriving) of the supercolony today shows, this would be only a palliative remediation, whose side effects are carried by the whole ecosystem of the Riviera, in which the usage of fertilizers, insecticides, and other polluting chemicals,

especially nitrates that contaminate the aquifers, is one of the problems connected to industrial floriculture.[15] A few years after Calvino's letter, denouncing
the complicity of science and technology with the pervasiveness of chemical
corporations in markets and environment, Rachel Carson would reveal the
lethality of modern insecticides, for which she has another name: "biocides"
(1962: 8). In *Silent Spring*, exhibiting the complex but unavoidable feedback
loop of chemicals, insect adaptation into "immune super races," and the creation
of ever-deadlier poisons, she would aver that "the chemical war is never won,
and all life is caught in its violent crossfire" (8). Writing a decade after *The
Argentine Ant*, Carson would show how, tempered by the abuse of chemicals in
agriculture and land management, the insects' threat only changes its face,
melding with larger and deeper environmental infiltrations. And she would go
on to hint at the parallel effect of radiation and pesticides on the evolution (and
perhaps even extinction) of our own species: "many chemicals, like radiation,
bring about gene mutations. It is ironic to think that man might determine his
own future by something so seemingly trivial as the choice of an insect spray"
(8).

Read in combination with *Silent Spring*, Calvino's *Argentine Ant* sounds
interestingly anticipatory. Moreover, Carson's passages on a techno-
contaminated evolutionary path resonate with Calvino's preoccupation with
the effects that atomic fallout might have on our genes. For instance, in *The
Watcher* (1963), faced with severe forms of disability, the protagonist openly
asks what happens to human genes in the long run when they are exposed to the
effects of invisible anthropogenic forces: how is "the material of the human
race" exposed to "the risk ... which is multiplied by the number of the new
snares: the viruses, poisons, uranium radiation" (Calvino 1971: 17–18)? Here
Calvino was explicit: this risk is not only a threat for individuals, but also
a "path evolution might yet take, ... if atomic radiations do act on the cells that
control the traits of the species" (21). In another prophetic novel, *Smog* (1958),
he even suspected that radiation might have an impact on the global climate.[16]

---

[15] See CeRSAA (undated).

[16] *Smog* is the story of a journalist working for an environmental magazine funded by a polluting
corporation. In a revelatory passage, the protagonist states: "The cloud of smog now seemed to
have grown smaller, a tiny little puff, a cirrus, compared to the looming atomic mushroom. ...
[Ev]ery day my eye fell upon statistics of terrible diseases, stories about fishermen overtaken in
the middle of the ocean by lethal clouds, guinea pigs born with two heads after some experiments
with uranium. ... The normal order of the seasons seemed changed, intense cyclones coursed
over Europe, the beginning of summer was marked by days heavily charged with electricity, then
by weeks of rain, by sudden heat waves and sudden resurgences of ... cold. The papers denied
that these atmospheric disorders could be in any way connected with the effects of the bomb;
only a few solitary scientists seemed to sustain this notion" (Calvino 1983a: 156). Although the
hypothesis that there might be links between global warming and atomic radiation is not

All this not only testifies to a comparable sensibility in interlacing science and literature, but also to the widespread debate on large-scale environmental concerns, in which Italo Calvino and his scientist parents were pioneering voices in Italy. From different angles and geographical standpoints, Calvino and Carson pinpoint one of the Anthropocene blind spots that we can clearly see today: the dark connection between these underground insect megacolonies, the global power of big chemical corporations, and us. Merging together history, nature, and Capital, this "monstrous" complex of factors can prompt us "to consider the wonders and terrors of symbiotic entanglement in the Anthropocene" (Swanson et al. 2017: M2). Seen in this light, the Argentine ant, with its massive global presence, appears almost like what Bruno Latour calls a "collective." Materializing in "the Ant," this collective is formed by a landscape and its underground side, the people who live there and their traffic, translocal ecosystemic connections, living species both vegetable and animal, transportation networks, chemicals, industry, global markets, the imagination of a young writer, and the garden of his parents. Emerging from this collective, the megacolony spreading from Liguria to Portugal is only one of the several territories conquered by the Argentine ant. This territory stretches from Australia to California, and includes the "smaller" Eastern Atlantic megacolonies, on one of which my kitchen pantry in Chapel Hill, currently facing an invasion of ants, is probably sitting. But it is perhaps inaccurate to talk about size: as recent studies report, the propagation has developed in such a way that "the global expansion of a single ant supercolony" might not be a literary hyperbole (Van Wilgenburg et al. 2010).

Before concluding this section, however, it would be interesting to examine this "symbiotic entanglement" from another perspective. The pervasive presence of the ant is also the epitome of how life itself interacts with geology in the Anthropocene. In its pathway of global expansion, *Linepithema humile* heavily transforms the underground, playing a role in what geologists call "bioturbation": a process through which "living organisms affect the substratum in (or on) which they live" (Kristensen et al. 2012: 285). Many animals are able to create this process. Think of beavers and rodents in general, earthworms, bacteria, or even plant roots that modify both bedrock and soil. Their impact on the subsurface ecosystems is so effective that they are called "ecosystem engineers" and "scenic designers, which not only set the stage, but also decide on the play to be performed, and select the potential players that enter the stage" (Meysman et al. 2006: 692). In principle, there is nothing unusual about this:

---

supported today by climatologists, the debate on possible climatic alterations, especially in the form of a "nuclear winter," has been a lively one for some time. See Iovino 2018.

underground landscapes coevolve with their biological residents. But the point, in *Linepithema*'s case, is that its bioturbulent presence has not coevolved with the local ecosystem, being rather the unwanted outcome of human intervention. Therefore, this apparently natural form of bioturbation is yet another expression of humanity's systemic interference. In other words, if ants have become monsters, "it is because of their entanglements – with us" (Swanson et al. 2017: M1). Among the "telluric actors," Serpil Oppermann observes, "the so-called anthropos ... is literally altering the foundational script itself .... Underlying global change, anthroturbation is the worst of all human induced alterations of the fabric of the Earth" (2018: 4–5). And this, of course, happens on all scales and in all realms, from gigantic ant colonies to the subterranean maps of colossal planetary extractivism.[17]

But the ants' behavior also prompts us to consider how naïve it is to think that purpose, strategic thinking, and even violence are features of our species alone. Behind the planetary success of the *Linepitema humilis* is, in fact, a particular genetic strategy. As ecologists Giraud, Pedersen, and Keller (2002: 6075) explain in their study on the Argentine ants of Southern Europe, the Mediterranean supercolony "effectively forms the largest cooperative unit ever recorded." This unit is composed of millions of nests and billions of individuals, displaying an enormously sophisticated system of collective agency based on pheromonal trail communication. All of these individuals are connected in a broad social structure with loose genetic relatedness called "unicoloniality," likely achieved through a mechanism of "genetic cleansing," that favors attachment to the community over genetic kinship. This makes the colony practically indestructible. Along with it, *Linepithema* possesses a highly effective mass recruitment system for ant workers and can face emergency situations in a very efficient way: "following environmental disturbances, such as flooding, Argentine ant workers relocate their entire colony to suitable nest sites via mass recruitment more quickly than other native ant species. Finally, during intraspecific aggressive encounters between Argentine ant supercolonies, enormous numbers of workers can be recruited to conflict zones" (Choe et al. 2012). Family bonds, in other words, are superseded by the affiliation of strangers that are forced into working for the colony collective. Here, zoosemiotical studies induce an interesting observation: if genetic bonds are not so important, it is because social insects such as ants are capable of cultural behaviors that, in order to enhance the structure of the colony, can be both intra- and interspecific, this latter including slaveism. As Dario Martinelli explains: "Although the intraspecific examples of cultural transmission are

---

[17] See Zalasiewicz et al. 2014 and Oppermann 2018.

certainly more recurrent in nature, it must be underlined that interspecific cases are far from rare, a most peculiar example being that of the so-called slaveism performed by certain species of ants on weaker species of insects" (2010: 203). And, in certain ant species, this cultural behavior goes so far as to include the skill to build tools, like the weaver ants *Oecophylla smaragdina*, that are able to "sew" leaves with a sort of silk secreted by a gland (276). Rather than a hyperobject, we could therefore say that "the Ant" is a hypersubject, prompting us to rethink the borders of nature and culture (and the scale of these very borders) in unprecedented ways.

Objects in the mirror, we are constantly reminded, are closer than they appear. Yet, here they are not only closer. They are already there – ant-shaped "strange strangers" that, in this very mirror, return our deformed image.[18] If *Anthropos* is altering the script of life, the magnitude of this alteration – call it Anthropocene, Plantationocene, or Capitalocene – is not a restatement of the superiority of human agency, but exactly the opposite: "No species, not even our own arrogant one pretending to be good individuals in so-called modern Western scripts, acts alone; assemblages of organic species and of abiotic actors make history, the evolutionary kind and the other kinds too," Donna Haraway writes (2016: 100). When "changes in degree" become "changes of kind," the scenery also changes. And, despite the optimism (or hubris) of their intentions, humans might be no longer at center stage.

The final scene of *The Argentine Ant*, as often happens in Calvino, is an expansion of the gaze. Zooming out from his own anguished situation like a drone hovering over Sanremo, the protagonist's attention embraces a landscape with other presences, other activities, other conversations, with stylistic accents and details that anticipate *Invisible Cities*. In the concluding lines, his gaze and the gaze of his wife linger on the sea, in a progression that moves from the surface to the bottom, where "there are no ants" and "the infinite grains of soft sand" mingle with the "white shells washed clean by the waves" (Calvino 1971: 180–181). It is a moment of "solastalgia": a nostalgia for the solace offered by a refuge of water that their home cannot be. A time will come when other aliens – microplastic, acids, the warming climate – will invade this watery asylum, creating another layer of the Anthropocene. But these are entanglements that Calvino, at that time, could not see.

3 Cats

Where is "nature" in the city? And is "nature" a refuge, or a place where alien presences gather, and ultimately turn against us? These questions, addressed

---

[18] On "strange strangers," see Morton 2011: 171 and passim.

time and again by Calvino, are the leitmotivs of *Marcovaldo, or the Seasons in the City*, perhaps his most popular narrative work in Italy, which he wrote and published over a period of eleven years, from 1952 to 1963. Reductively considered to be a children's book (a label that its author only partially accepted and that I would like to disprove), *Marcovaldo* tells the year-round adventures of a poor, working-class man trapped in an unspecified "industrial city," where he ardently – and yet unsuccessfully – "looks for 'nature'" (Calvino 2003: I, 1233). What he finds, instead, are the problematic urban embodiments of this "nature": poisonous mushrooms at the bus stop, fish contaminated by chemicals, mutant plants, overly aggressive wasps, snow tainted by soot... Threatened and threatening, this nature is "mischievous, counterfeit, compromised with artificial life" (I, 1233). This is another way of saying that it is, intrinsically, an alien nature – and hardly a refuge. In these twenty stories, five for each season, overlapping niches and spaces, encounters and partitions, competition and cooperation, are repeatedly investigated, criticized, and reinvented, in the search for more inclusive – yet not unproblematic – multispecies geometries of life.[19]

There is an exemplary place, in Marcovaldo's city, where these dynamics are more visible. It is a curious garden where felines rule over and even dominate their human neighbors. Numerous and fiery, hungry for food and space, these cats not only compete with people for both, but form an inaccessible colony wherein the city seems to take another shape and speak another language. Such are the premises of "The Garden of Stubborn Cats" (1963), one of the most puzzling and visionary episodes of the collection, and the perfect epitome for the second site of our constellation of Anthropocene life-systems: the industrial city. The plot reminds us at once of a folktale and a surrealist story. Following a tabby that has stolen a trout from him (a trout that he had previously stolen from a restaurant), Marcovaldo stumbles into a messy patch, infested by cats. The garden surrounds a dilapidated villa belonging to an old marquise. Badly off and forlorn, the lady would like to yield the property to the pressing requests of building developers, but the cats' hostility systematically prevents her from doing so. The woman eventually dies, the lot is acquired, and the house is demolished. Until the end, however, the feline colony – like the Argentine ant, another collective organism – claims possession of the place, disturbing the construction site in many ways – and yet strangely managing to keep it "naturally" alive with frogs, birds, and other feral animals.

---

[19] For ecocritical readings of *Marcovaldo*, see Ross 2003; Matiassi Cantarin and Marino 2018; Sanna 2018.

Within a few, intensely imaginative pages, Calvino recapitulates some of the key principles (and problems) of commensalism and urban ecology, playing with the intermittently undomesticated nature of cats – these "mysteriously familiar" critters whose evolution still embeds enigmatic zones.[20] And a "next-door" ecological mystery is indeed the cipher of this episode. Bossy, secretive, naughty, the "stubborn cats" seem to belong to a society of their own, oftentimes parallel to and competing with the human one. Real complicity with them, Marcovaldo learns, is an illusion. Even when he thinks he has "penetrated the secrecy of the felines' society," he has to admit that "their realm [has] territories, ceremonies, customs that it [is] not yet granted to him to discover" (1983b: 102–103).

Although not as alien as the Argentine ant, cats look pretty much like aliens, in this story. And perhaps one of the reasons for their foreignness is the difficulty of ultimately pigeonholing them as either wild or domesticated (which is also biologically true: *Felis catus silvestris* and *Felis catus domesticus* are two different species, yet they interbreed to fertile offspring).[21] Discussing the structure of "agrilogistics" – the logic of earth manipulation underlying the Anthropocene – Timothy Morton emphasizes the "ambiguous status of cats" in relation to our species. Their condition, he provocatively claims, "is not quite the 'companion species' Haraway thinks through human coexistence with dogs" (Morton 2016: 49). Tame and yet irreducible to any form of control, cats "stand for the ontological ambiguity of lifeforms and indeed of things at all. Cats are a *neighbor* species. . . . The penetrating gaze of a cat is used as the gaze of the extraterrestrial alien because cats are the *intraterrestrial* alien. Cats just happen" (Morton 2016: 49). Intraterrestrial aliens, odd ontological neighbors, cats "just happen" – and are as elusive and unknowable as "things" are: this is how the champion of object-oriented-ontology sees them, and this is how Marcovaldo seems to perceive them, too. Still, whether or not as companion species (which they are, in fact), cats have been living alongside humans for millennia, and their association with us dates back to the beginning of the Holocene. The process of domestication probably occurred about 12,000–9,000 years ago, when the forerunners of the modern tabbies started hanging around farming communities in the Fertile Crescent (the Levant, Southern Turkey, and Iraq).[22] Attracted by the abundance of prey and food around cereal stocking sites, wildcats "invaded and colonised Neolithic towns and villages whose human inhabitants immediately saw the benefits of allowing these

---

[20] On cats as "mysteriously familiar," see O'Connor 2013: 57. On the evolution of felines, see, among others, Serpell 1996 and 2014: 13–18 and passim.
[21] O'Connor 2013: 58.
[22] The ancestor of cats is considered to be *Felis catus Lybica*. See Ottoni et al. 2016.

animals to live around their rodent-infested homes and granaries" (Serpell 2014: 87). From patrolling granaries to eating scraps of human food, the step is not that long – and here what life scientists call "commensalism" emerges: a relationship between two species, in which one benefits from the other without necessarily returning the same kind of favor to (but also without harming) its "host" (see O'Connor 2013). As for dogs, pigs, and other proximal nonhumans, it is through this bond based on opportunism or vicinity that the domestication of cats began. Unlike their "tamed colleagues," however, felines appear to have displayed from the outset a certain degree of independence: cats, in other words, are believed to have "domesticated themselves," profiting from the opportunity to find shelter and obtain food around humans in many ways, including (obviously!) deliberate handouts.[23] As zooarcheologists have shown, in early agricultural settlements cats already played a variety of roles, "ranging from mutualistic hunters and scavengers to encouraged animals or even pets" (Hu et al. 2014).

Of course, when food is scarce commensalism might turn into antagonism, and this is exactly what happens in *Marcovaldo*. A poignant example is the scene with the trout. Stolen by Marcovaldo, the fish first ends up in a "banquet" of cats, and finally in the frying pan of the old lady whose villa is under feline siege. Here, in particular, the competition over the same meal – itself a creature whose hopelessness and subjectivity Calvino carefully describes (1983b: 105) – demonstrates how living beings are alike in their struggle for survival: a constant in *Marcovaldo*, there are no differences of species among marginal beings, especially in modern urban contexts. In this episode, however, the story of commensalism and biosocial marginality is also the story of the ambivalent status of urban cats, often split between pets and unauthorized presences.[24] Even more, it is the story of how high a toll the development of the industrial city has imposed upon the feral existence of these evolutionary comrades of ours. It is in this makeover of ecologies and landscapes – which involves the materialization of threats, obstacles, and hegemonic spaces – that the fissure between the worlds of humans and cats opens. As Calvino writes in one of his most memorable passages:

---

[23] Todd 1978. Developing Todd's research, O'Connor (2013, 59) remarks that "there was no credible process by which people could have deliberately initiated and managed the domestication of cats, and little reason for people to have done so. Thus . . . the impetus for cats to adopt a commensal habit must have come from cats exploiting the feeding and shelter opportunities offered by human settled communities." On "Commensal Species," see also O'Connor 2017.

[24] This latter detail would prompt a reflection about the not always humane history of animal sheltering and the pain often inflicted on dogs and cats freely roaming in urban spaces, many of whom were and still are impounded and killed. In the recent past, stray animals (including many lost but unclaimed pets) were usually employed in medical research. See Irvine 2017.

> The city of cats and the city of men exist one inside the other, but they are not
> the same city. Few cats recall the time when there was no distinction ... But
> for several generations now domestic felines have been prisoners of an
> uninhabitable city: the streets are uninterruptedly overrun by the mortal
> traffic of cat-crushing automobiles; in every square foot of terrain where
> once a garden extended or a vacant lot ... now condominiums loom up ... the
> courtyards ... have been roofed by reinforced concrete and transformed into
> garages ... But in ... this compressed city ... a kind of counter-city opens,
> a negative city ... it is a city of cavities, wells, air conduits, ... like a network
> of dry canals on a planet of stucco and tar, and it is through this network,
> grazing the walls, that the ancient cat population still scurries. (1983b: 101)

It has often been observed that the garden of stubborn cats is perhaps
Calvino's first "invisible city": a "thin" feline city, squeezed by the "continuous" (and indifferent) "city of men." In this dual picture, a bulky, implacable
body of concrete tramples the airy matter of another possibility of living,
forcing it to retreat into leftover interstices, the "empty slices between wall
and wall" (101). Here, casual architectural elements are jumbled with fragments
of life and time, cars and concrete collide with the habits embedded in the cats'
feral genes, and there is no place for "vacant" spots or refuges. Confined in a city
within a city, a city that they inhabit inside a city that does not recognize – or
even see – their presence, the cats populate what Michel Foucault would call
a "heterotopia": a place "other," which is absolutely real and yet elsewhere –
almost cast out – from reality, a mirror that at the same time duplicates reality
and transforms it into its absence. There is a particular feature in these "alter-
places," Foucault maintains. Unlike utopias, which only exist outside the actual
world, heterotopias are in fact physical spaces: prisons, hospitals, cemeteries,
asylums, boarding schools. They are "a kind of both mythical and real contestation of the space in which we live" (1997: 350). The garden, as "the smallest
fragment of the world and, at the same time, [representing] its totality," is one of
them, too (350).

A material discourse of contestation and survival, the garden of the stubborn
cats is heterotopic. It is mythical like a past of nontraumatic coexistence too far
back for us to remember, and yet real like the "network of dry canals on a planet
of stucco and tar" that signals the level of compression to which life – all life – is
subjected in the "continuous" megacity which our planet has become.[25]

This is a story of ambiguity that might very well apply to the situation of cats
in our cities: although cats on earth have never been as numerous as they are
today, being like dogs and other pets at the center of a huge global business, their
management still raises challenging questions of violence, justice, and even

---

[25] Since 2008, more than the 50 percent of the world's population live in cities. See Dawson 2017.

biopolitics.[26] In particular, feline colonies are considered more of a problem in cities, where "controlling efforts" go from milder techniques such as "desexing" to the most radical "culling," namely capturing and killing.[27] The underlying problem, however, is that modern cities are dangerous for every interstitial being, and above all for feral animals. For example, as a study on bird mortality in the United States has shown, between 500 million to more than 1 billion birds are killed every year by anthropogenic causes, including "collisions with human-made structures such as vehicles, buildings and windows, power lines, communication towers, and wind turbines; electrocutions; oil spills and other contaminants; pesticides."[28] As has been observed, the social dynamics that, following the processes of capital accumulation, have transformed the urban space since the nineteenth century, have also "transformed interspecies relations, forcing nonhuman animals to navigate unchecked emissions, polluted waterways, rapid urban development, and landscapes of resource extraction" (Owens and Wolch 2017, 548–549). And the other side of the coin is represented here by those animals that, due to the disappearance of their habitat, are forced to move to cities: browsers such as deer, predators such as skunks, raccoons, possums, coyotes, snakes... For them, "synanthropic or synurbanic life often means protection from predation and plentiful food," but it is also a source of serious "ecological or evolutionary 'traps'" (Owens and Wolch 2017, 553–554).

This loss of feral habitats is clearly a "mild apocalypse," and the tale of the two cities in *Marcovaldo* is a poignant example of this fact.[29] But what does this apocalypse at once reveal and mourn? Readable in the retreating spaces of the cats' "negative city," the answer to this question induces a reflection about the Holocene–Anthropocene shift. And this reflection, articulated in indirect conversation by Anna Tsing and Donna Haraway, is illuminating to understand what I consider to be the key point of "The Garden of Stubborn Cats." As Tsing

---

[26] Donna Haraway, whose pages on the market and the commodification of dogs (and pets in general) as "lively capital" are an unmatched reference (2008, 45–69), writes that, in that they undergo surgery and vaccination, cats are "interpellated into the modern biopolitical state" (277). Chapter 11 of *When Species Meet*, "Becoming Companion Species in Technoculture," offers insightful considerations and kinship stories that can be fruitfully read vis-à-vis episodes from *Marcovaldo* (Haraway 2008). See also the section on Labs.

[27] The world's cat population is estimated to be more than a half billion worldwide; see Hu et al. 2014. As the Australian Pet Welfare Foundation reports, today every second dog and 85–95 percent of cats are unnecessarily killed in pounds (see https://petwelfare.org.au/2017/07/03/9-steps-zero/). On the situation of "urban animals" in Italy, see the report of the NGO Legambiente, *Animali in città* (Morabito 2016). Interestingly, one of the cities with the largest rate of feline colonies per resident is Sanremo, with one cat for every fifteen people (16).

[28] Wallace et al. 2005: 1029. It has also to be acknowledged that domestic cats are among the most effective urban predators in killing a huge number of birds and native rodents.

[29] "Mild apocalypse" comes from Bubandt and Tsing 2018: 2.

writes in an article titled "A Threat to Holocene Resurgence is a Threat to Livability" (2017), the Holocene was an age in which, following coevolutionary patterns, the earth was a place of refuge for many species, including ours. In this epoch, despite the massive spread of humans at the expense of other species, "human farming managed to co-exist with a wide variety of other living beings" (54). The Holocene was, in other words, a time of "multispecies assemblages" whose mutual connections were strengthened by the existence of *refugia*: places where communities of diverse species could be restored after major events (desertification, clearcutting, etc.) and periods of cold or drought induced by the Ice Age glaciation (54). In these life-spaces, with or without humans in the picture, different critters could prosper and biodiverse encounters could be enabled. Not yet turned into forms of "human disturbance," Holocene farming was therefore not antagonistic to nonhuman expansion, and in fact helped the animals and plants threatened by adverse environmental conditions to survive, recover, and thrive together. Things changed when the multispecies collectives of Holocene farming were wiped out by the massive ecologies of human proliferation that characterize the Anthropocene. As Donna Haraway writes, "the Holocene was the long period when refugia, places of refuge, still existed, even abounded, to sustain reworlding in rich cultural and biological diversity." With the capitalist "cheapening" of nature, however, the reserves necessary to sustain this "reworlding" have been "drained, burned, depleted, poisoned, exterminated, and otherwise exhausted."[30] Seen in this light, the Anthropocene is therefore the end of refugia – the end of habitats, the end of *oikos*. But the life-space fragmentation touches not only feral species or nonhuman beings: "Right now, the earth is full of refugees, human and not, without refuge" (Haraway 2016: 100).

If we relate this discourse to *Marcovaldo*'s episode, we can see that once again, with the apparent lightness of irony, that Calvino was making an important point: he was not simply asking, with Marcovaldo himself, "where is 'nature' in the industrial city?" but, most urgently, is there any space left for unprotected natures in the industrial city? Where, in the city, are the harbors left for refugees – human and nonhuman – without refuge? Marcovaldo's city, indeed, is the epitome of this time and space wherein the "the dream/nightmare of a hyper-separated nature" (Rose et al. 2017: 5) is shattered in front of the impossibility of really keeping the consequences of such hyper-separation within the limits of our control. Observed more closely, then, this episode is not simply the story of a clash between species (albeit evolutionary kin), but

---

[30] Haraway 2016: 100. See also Dawson 2016.

another Anthropocene story. It is indeed a story of hegemonic spaces, of critical zones of survival, of disappearing refuges.

The last remaining outpost of a feral community, the marquise's garden is thus literally a Holocene refuge: although apparently "alien," with their uncanny collective agency, these cats are in fact refugees. Yet, "the ancient cat population still scurries," in this interstitial dimension. And, at the end of the story, it becomes stubbornly generative:

> In the spring, instead of the garden, there was a huge building site ... The steam shovels dug down to great depths to make room for the foundations, cement poured into the iron armatures ... But [c]ats walked along all the planks, they made bricks fall and upset buckets of mortar, they fought in the midst of the piles of sand. When you started to raise an armature, you found a cat perched on the top of it, hissing fiercely. ... And the birds continued making their nests in all the trestles, the cab of the crane looked like an aviary ... And you couldn't dip up a bucket of water that wasn't full of frogs, croaking and hopping ... (Calvino 1983b: 111)

The last undomesticated spot amidst a forest of concrete, the garden becomes a sanctuary for anarchic natures, where hundreds of cats (and birds, rats, frogs, insects, wild plants ...) gather and settle. The place is a refuge for all the pariah-critters surviving in the industrial city, an involuntary reservation wherein the invisible natures/refugees that struggle to live in "the city of men" continue to exist despite the incorporating encroachment of *Anthropos*. Here the cats resist, haunting the site not with their ghosts but with their raids and tenacious presence, thus turning the "only undeveloped bit of land in the downtown area" (108) into a "jardin de résistance" – a garden of resistance, as the French landscape theorist Gilles Clément would call it.

"'Feral,'" Donna Haraway writes, "is another name for contingent 'becoming with' for all the actors" (2008: 281). In the interlaced fates of this "ferality tale," Calvino gives us a minuscule but significant testimony of multispecies ethnography, namely an "account of a way of life" which is no longer exclusively related to the human but heeds all the bonds that make life possible in a shared biocultural dimension. Focusing on the predicaments that take place inside and around this garden (and having a human like Marcovaldo in the picture), Calvino is describing the cross-species "experience of life within a world of meaning, generating empathy as well as understanding."[31] In these pages (and in *Marcovaldo* more generally), he adopts a perspective which, productively fluctuating between humans and nonhumans, allows him to imagine extended forms of subjectivity, struggle, and desire that exhibit the mutual creation (we

---

[31] Quotes from Rose 2015: 110. On "ferality tales" see Garrard 2014.

might say, ecopolitical "symbiogenesis") of all the "citizens" living in this problematically shared space.[32] If we look into the Greek roots of the word "ethnography," we find therein a form of storytelling, of handing down stories (*grapho*, write), and, evoked by *ethnos*, "a multitude (whether of men or of beasts) associated or living together; a company, troop, or swarm of individuals of the same nature or genus."[33] This tells us a lot about how the human, both as an organism and as a social being, emerges from and with this swarming multitude. Yet, the relevant issue might be another: "Rather than simply celebrate multispecies mingling, ethnographers have begun to explore a central question: Who benefits, cui bono, when species meet?"[34] It is both hard and simple to answer this question, in the Anthropocene. Certainly, the Holocene adventure of humans and felines shows that this benefit can indeed be mutual: in early agricultural settlements, the cats received shelter and food, providing an environment free from rodents in return. Just around the corner from the Holocene, however, "The Garden of the Stubborn Cats" also exposes how complicated it is to keep in place the multispecies entanglements that sustained our kinships and companionships. But the end of this mutual exchange also redefines the species identity of the human as something which is very diverse in itself. This short episode tells us that humans, too, are residents in this feline city: marginal humans that, like Marcovaldo, struggle to find their place within the exclusionary territories of a new epoch. And so, if cats lose their refuge and place in the city of humans, it is because this city does not belong to individual and "ordinary" humans anymore, but to *Anthropos*: the disembodied corporate subject that fills cities with concrete, factories, and hegemonic spaces. *Anthropos* impacts both the earth's dynamics and the earthlings' communities, and it is perhaps the only one to benefit from the ending of refuges and contact zones. In the new landscape of this epoch, along with contact zones, all the entanglements that made the human life possible as a multispecies event are at stake, too. And Calvino knows that. *Anthropos*, not cat or even ant, is the name of the alien.

This "corporate subject" is anything but an abstraction. In fact, it is the very embodiment of the inequities that trouble the contemporary ecologies of life, both human and nonhuman. One of the most problematic questions about the "Sixth Extinction" is its mere definition as "anthropogenic." Mass extinction – like all processes that radically alter the biosphere – is not abstractly caused by "the human." As Deborah Bird Rose, Matthew Chrulew, and Thom van Dooren write, "radical inequity and highly differential positioning are the name of the

---

[32] On the concept of symbiogenesis and its application to the discourse of multispecies ethnography, see Margulis 1998.

[33] Grimm et al. 1887: 168, quoted and discussed in Kirksey 2014: 1.   [34] Kirksey et al. 2014: 2.

game": not only are we called to investigate the loss of nonhuman species and the loss of refuges, but also "the many ways in which human communities are affected by and suffer through extinction" as well as "the specific political, economic, and cultural forms of human organization most responsible for any given extinction. ... Excavating this specificity matters" (2017: 6). If we excavate this specificity, Calvino suggests, we find building developers, agricultural landscapes converted into monocultures, industrialists who own polluting factories as well as information channels, and all the rippling iniquities of a hierarchic society. It is *Anthropos* qua Capital that drives the city of cats away from the city of humans – and that reduces the refuges available for Marcovaldo and other animals. In the split between these two cities is the crisis of the refugees of the industrial city, the crisis of beings that have lost their habitats, the desperation of nonhumans that are bereft of their space for living. And, impossible to forget, here is also the desperation of more and more humans who, as the crisis of homelessness in all the world's big cities intensifies, lose their living spaces.

This is something that prompts us to reconsider the notion of companion species, exactly as a category that could at the same time question and stop the confinement of the "others" enacted by *Anthropos*. As Haraway reminds us, in fact, "The discursive tie between the colonized, the enslaved, the noncitizen, and the animal – all reduced to type, all Others to rational man, and all essential to his bright constitution – is at the heart of racism and flourishes, lethally, in the entrails of humanism" (2008: 18). Creating coalitions (which might be historical or evolutionary) between "noncitizens" (which might be human or nonhuman) is the response to the homogeneity of species, class, and all sort of socially constructed "ontological" boundaries. By putting a marginal citizen like Marcovaldo in close (yet problematic) companionship with an "urban colony" of cats, Calvino offers a creative and generative example of beings that did "learn to live intersectionally" (Haraway 2008: 18), implicitly providing a response to all exclusionary logics of an *Anthropos*-centered society.

But we can also reverse this discourse into a positive reflection about citizenship. If there is a city of cats, Calvino implicitly suggests, then cats are also citizens. This is the idea of a "multinatural metropolis" or "zoöpolis" that, soliciting a rethinking of urban governance in the light of the twentieth-century animal rights movement and of what we know about animal subjectivity, questions traditional notions of citizenship. Including nonhumans in decision-making processes about natural resources, land transformation, and other critical actions becomes inescapable: "Animals should enjoy rights to the city, and the city, in turn, should, where possible, offer them shelter, sustenance, and safe passage" (Owens and Wolch 2017: 559).

This is the lesson to be drawn from Marcovaldo's story. We should perhaps refocus our gaze and start seeing the city itself as a big organism, populated by sparse feral presences that we often ignore. Many are the cities that, along with the city of cats, we don't see within the "city of men": these are the cities of birds, of ants, bees, bugs, frogs, bats, reptiles, of impounded dogs, of industrially farmed cattle, of caged rabbits and mice in a lab ... All these are invisible cities, too – or cities that we will never be able to see, considering how fast many of these creatures, especially insects, are disappearing in the Anthropocene. *Marcovaldo* is a reflection on the political ecology of the city, on its social biodiversity and multispecies justice, on its plural ontologies, on its stratification – of air, buildings, colors, food, society, and species. There is nothing more reductive than trying to explain this work only in terms of a "modernist parable" of the "industrial-style" *bon sauvage*. *Marcovaldo* is much more than that. It is a treatise on urban ecology, with all its issues of space, life, evolution, separation, contamination, justice, energy, resources, health, and imagination. Telling the stories of little "gardens of resistance," refuges carved in the megacity, is a way to cultivate windows of hope in which all forms of life are engaged. In looking for "nature" in the industrial city, Marcovaldo is perhaps only trying to trace the human back to its root: that of the coincidence with humus, the dark, fermenting life of the soil that connects us, materially, evolutionarily, and emotionally, with all the rest.

4 The Rabbit

As "The Garden of the Stubborn Cats" clearly suggested, Marcovaldo's industrial city is the prelude to that storied universe suspended between imagination and very concrete urban ecologies that will materialize in Calvino's *Invisible Cities*. Anticipating these visionary (and perhaps prophetic) landscapes dominated by waste, memories, and things, Marcovaldo's city is an indefinite ecological continuum oozing singularities, with many neglected and yet eloquent corners: abandoned grounds, feral bus stops where mushrooms grow, imperceptibly polluted water streams, fuliginous rooftops, mysterious outskirts, and labyrinthine supermarkets. All of these spots host yet more stories and unexpected adventures. Their coprotagonist is what Calvino calls "nature": a word that in this context means everything that challenges the lifeless arrangements and constraints of the industrial world, in a tragicomic choreography that includes Marcovaldo and his family. The hospital – with its atmosphere halfway between salvation and reclusion – is one of the most problematic and enigmatic of these corners. There are dark corners hidden inside this corner, too, and the lab is the hidden corner par excellence. A typically cordoned space in which only scientists and "test subjects" are allowed, it is quintessentially off-limits to the public gaze. Or rather, it would be, if an accidental and yet particularly sensible visitor had not broken the cordon and lifted the veil on this place and its unfortunate residents. This is what Marcovaldo, in the double function of victim (consistently) and perpetrator (tentatively), does in the episode titled "The Poisonous Rabbit." Once again by way of a narrative dressed in tones of irony and fable, the kinship of substances and treatments between human and nonhuman bodies is revealed. And once again Marcovaldo acts as a litmus-test character, a diffractive instrument through which all the inconsistencies, aspirations, and conflicts of a malfunctioning natural–cultural aggregate are brought to light.

The story opens with Marcovaldo being released from hospital, where he has spent a few days recovering from an unspecified illness. While he is about to leave the sanatorium – a place where everything reminds him of "torture or discomfort" (Calvino 1983b: 52) – he spots a white rabbit in a cage. Bony underneath the fluffy coat, with his "amazed red eyes" and his "ears almost furless flattened against its back," the rabbit is hungry and scared. Taking advantage of the doctor's absence, Marcovaldo snatches the animal and brings him home to his family. In doing so, his attitude is ambivalent: if the immediate connection with the rabbit makes him feel his desolation, thinking "of how unhappy the animal must be, shut up in there" (52), Marcovaldo's purpose is, undeniably, also that of eating him. Once at home, however, no one has the courage to kill the bunny. In fact, the children immediately welcome him as their pal, and take him up to the house terrace, where they start playing together. All of a sudden, an ambulance siren reveals the danger: "injected . . . with the germs of a terrible disease," the rabbit has become "poisonous" (54). Desperately, the animal struggles to escape from the crew of doctors, policemen, and Red Cross volunteers who have precipitously come to fetch him. In a final moment of self-determination, the rabbit tries to commit suicide, throwing himself from the rooftops, but he lands "in the gloved hands of a fireman" (59). Frustrated even in this "extreme act of animal dignity," he is hustled into an ambulance, which brings him back to the hospital. And aboard the ambulance is also Marcovaldo, this time with his entire family: they will be all "interned for observation and for a series of vaccine tests" (59).

"The Poisonous Rabbit" is a biopolitical game of mirrors and Russian dolls. The complexity of this episode is in the circuit of ambivalences, echoes, and reversed realities, culminating with the *mise-en-abyme* of spaces and subjectivities around which the story is articulated. A distressed patient, Marcovaldo perceives the hospital not simply as a site of cure, but also of anxiety and even "torture" (52). Waiting to leave this place of temporary captivity, in a segment of the sanatorium which almost recalls a circle of Dante's inferno, he recognizes in the rabbit another patient, this time literally embodying the agony expressed by this word, whose Greek root *path-* indicates both "suffering" and "passiveness." Like him, the rabbit-patient is indeed a *passive* being in the hands of impersonal actors. Unlike him, however, *this* patient does not undergo any therapeutic treatment. The rabbit, therefore, *suffers* both cognitively and existentially. Unable to understand the reasons for his torturous detention in a cage-within-a-cage, the animal is absorbing in his body all the predicaments of this obscure mechanism. Enclosed in the same place, and yet not caught in the same situation, human and nonhuman patients incarnate respectively the bright and dark side of pharmaceutical practice: cure and poisoning. Yet, each are literally *patients*: passive subjects in the hands of a system incapable of seeing them.

An interface between these dimensions, Marcovaldo is perfectly aware of this situation. Like him, the rabbit is swallowed by the medical institution, which is swallowed in turn by the industrial landscape of the city. This leads to a consideration, pivotal for the Anthropocene discourse, on the "economy of space" of these oppressive relationships. Laboratories, like breeding stations, fill "a whole hidden geography . . . wherein many animals live and die as part of a highly unequal human-animal relation predicated on the utility, adaptability and expendability of the animals so incarcerated. Questions about science, state intervention (or lack of it) and capitalist industry are obviously again to the fore, as well as those of ethics, welfare and politics." Instead of being "tucked away in countryside complexes and university campuses," in *Marcovaldo* this "hidden geography" is located right in the heart of the city. Unlike the other sites of animal production and forced reproduction, which are to be found in the peripheral circuits of the "industrial countryside," here the lab is placed within one of the city's central institutions. A box within a box, the lab is in fact a secret hidden in plain sight, exactly like the many facets of "capitalist industry" that are incorporated in our cities, bodies, and everyday life habits, all of them with their issues of "ethics, welfare, and politics."[35]

In the city, different species only meet in the framework of codified relationships, which are more or less instrumental or mediated. Spontaneous encounters might still come about in the liminal zones that have heroically (or accidentally) escaped from the narrative of development. This happens with the cats in the old lady's garden. But rabbits, unlike cats, are not feral presences, in an urban

---

[35] Quotes from Philo and Wilbert 2000: 2. By inviting us to visualize the animal body as a crossroad of "corporeality, substances, and physical agencies," Stacy Alaimo also insists that "animals need to be considered within material systems – not only within ecosystems and habitats but also within food systems, big pharma, chemical industries, and other areas of global capitalism" (2015: 12).

environment: by discovering the animal on his way home, Marcovaldo sadly knows that, in "the foggy city" outside the hospital "you don't encounter rabbits" (52). Yet, *inside* the hospital, this rabbit is "a friendly presence, which would have sufficed to fill [Marcovaldo's] hours and his thoughts" as a lonesome patient (52). Perceived as a companion animal, potentially offering the chance of a mutual relationship, the rabbit is able to respond to one of Marcovaldo's deepest and most spontaneous existential needs: the need for affective proximity – the feeling that underlies the "force of encounter," as affect theorists call it.[36]

A brotherly presence encapsulated in the map of pain, the rabbit is, therefore, an emotional mirror for Marcovaldo.[37] This experience of proximity is enabled by the view of the animal's body: a body that, like Marcovaldo's body, feels. The body here becomes a vehicle for a radical sympathy, which enacts the etymological meaning of "suffering" (*pathos*, again) "together" (*syn*-). The philosopher Ralph Acampora has called this specular feeling *symphysis*: an embodied form of cross-species care that propagates from common physical experiences (2006: 23). Acampora defines this a "corporal compassion," an existential condition of mutual "vulnerability and togetherness" (122) that is correlate to a shared sensibility and an "ethical sensorium" (117). Inspired by the phenomenology of Maurice Merleau-Ponty, this approach describes the human/nonhuman relationship as a mutual coming into contact of sensibilities and subjectivities, in which identity emerges as a form of "inter-animality."[38] Feminist philosopher Lori Gruen adds to this concept yet another layer: that of "entangled empathy" – an ethical approach based on a process that involves "a particular blend of affection and cognition" (2015, 66). Through this process we "perceive and . . . connect with a specific other in their particular circumstance" (67), becoming responsive to their needs, interests, vulnerabilities, desires, fears, and hopes.

---

[36] "Companion animal" is how Linzey and Linzey (2018: 19) refer to animal friends or pets. I am deliberately not using Haraway's notion of companion species here, in order to emphasize the singularity of the encounter. On "the force of encounter," see Seigworth and Gregg 2010: 2. By noticing that the rabbit, like all the nonhuman presences in Marcovaldo's city, is a personification of that "nature" constantly chased after by the protagonist, it is also important to observe that Calvino's attitude here resonates with Jennifer Wolch's idea that "concrete interactions and interdependence with animal others are indispensable to the development of human cognition, identity, and consciousness, and to a maturity that accepts ambiguity, difference, and lack of control" (1998, 122). This would be, she maintains, the very core of an urban ecology called "Zoöpolis," based on human/nonhuman noncompetitive interactions.

[37] Sympathy for the rabbit, Ross observes, signifies "a direct identification with the captive creature, for on several occasions Marcovaldo himself is portrayed as a prisoner of the industrial city" (2003, 32).

[38] On this topic, see Westling 2013.

The density of this "inter-animal" encounter is premised on the underlying motive – almost a *basso continuo* – of this short story: the exposure of the rabbit to torment, fear, and deception. From Calvino's narrative it is evident that, although the animal cannot explain or understand these experiences, he perfectly feels and *knows* them. In a passage to which we will return later, Calvino writes that the rabbit

> *knew* that every time humans tried to attract [him] with offers of food, something obscure and painful happened: either they stuck a syringe into [his] flesh, or a scalpel, or they forced [him] into a buttoned-up jacket . . . And the *memory* of these misfortunes merged with the *pain* [he] felt inside, with the slow change of organs that [he] *sensed*, with the *prescience* of death. (58, my emphases)

The rabbit, despite his forced passivity, is the active subject of an embodied form of cognition.

In his seminal book *The Case for Animal Rights* (1983), Tom Regan described animals like Marcovaldo's rabbits as "moral patients," or "subjects-of-a-life" – namely, nonhuman creatures "who have desires and beliefs, who perceive, remember, and can act intentionally, who have a sense of the future, including their own future (i.e., are self-aware or self-conscious), who have an emotional life, who have a psychophysical identity over time, who have a kind of autonomy (namely, preference-autonomy), and who have an experiential welfare" (153; see also 243). Written in 1954, "The Poisonous Rabbit" pioneeringly deals, therefore, with crucial issues that will come to the forefront of the debate on applied ethics only in the early 1970s, with books such as Peter Singer's *Animal Liberation* (1975) and Regan's treatise on animal rights (1983).[39] These issues are the cruelty of animal testing, vivisection, and the imprisonment and harming of sentient beings: standardized practices in a way of doing scientific research flattened on a graphic extremization of Cartesian dualism. Such practices are de facto the defining features of nonhuman treatment in the industrial era, whereby the recognition of animals as sentient beings – not to mention their moral considerability – is only an obstruction to their massive use as tools and disposable resources.[40]

---

[39] On the date of composition and publication of "The Poisonous Rabbit," see Calvino 2003: I, 1367, 1384.

[40] The debate on animal ethics in its early phases has a glorious history that I can only render here with a bird's eye view on its milestones. One is the publication, in 1971, of *Animals, Men and Morals: An Inquiry into the Maltreatment of Non-humans* edited by Stanley and Roslind Godlovitch, and John Harris, three young philosophers working in Oxford. In a chapter of this book, written by the clinical psychologist Richard D. Ryder, the word "speciesism" appears for the first time. Another milestone is Peter Singer's *Animal Liberation* (1975), which confronts speciesism and anthropocentrism in western ethics by embracing a utilitarian perspective

A look at the historical context will help us appreciate the groundbreaking originality of Calvino's stance. Of course, the issue of the humane treatment of animals dates back to the eighteenth century, and literature had already dealt with the pain that modernity inflicts onto them. In Italy, for example, a unique case of literary representation of animal tests is the chapter "Febo" in Curzio Malaparte's famous novel *La pelle* (*The Skin*, 1949), wherein the author describes, in excruciating detail, the agony of a dog, captured and used in vivisection experiments.[41] However, animal welfare really became a political question at the end of the 1950s, when the use of lab animals and industrial farming reached massive proportions. The official inception of this debate is conventionally identified with the publication of the Brambell Report, commissioned and released by the UK government in 1965. The document was the result of a scientific investigation, directed by Professor Francis W. Rogers Brambell, about the safety of intensively farmed animals, partly as a response to concerns raised in 1964 by the activist and writer Ruth Harrison in a popular book titled *Animal Machines*. Even though the primary responsibility of the Report was "[t]o examine the conditions in which livestock are kept under systems of intensive husbandry and to advise whether standards ought to be set in the interests of their welfare, and if so what they should be," its scope also extended to animal testing (Brambell 1965: 1). The Report, which "was the first formal recognition by an official body" of nonhuman suffering, was conducive to the formulation of the famous "Five Freedoms":

> Freedom from hunger or thirst by ready access to fresh water and a diet to maintain full health and vigor; Freedom from discomfort by providing an appropriate environment including shelter and a comfortable resting area; Freedom from pain, injury or disease by prevention or rapid diagnosis and treatment; Freedom to express (most) normal behaviour by providing sufficient space, proper facilities and company of the animal's own kind; Freedom from fear and distress by ensuring conditions and treatment which avoid mental suffering.[42]

In "The Poisonous Rabbit," quite surprisingly, the bunny is denied all these freedoms before they were even formulated as such. Marcovaldo is aware of that as well, and empathizes with him. Let us reexamine their first encounter:

---

derived from the philosophy of Jeremy Bentham. Bringing Singer's philosophy even further, Tom Regan (1983) advocates for a nonutilitarian theory of animal rights.

[41] On the history of human–animal relations in modern Europe, see Keith Thomas's landmark study *Man and the Natural World* (1983). One of the first modern novels to expose the cruelty of the meat industry is Upton Sinclair's *The Jungle* (1906), whose focus falls, however, more strongly on the inhuman conditions of meatpacking workers.

[42] Quotes from Wilkie 2017: 282, and Farm Animal Welfare Council (n.d.). On this issue, see also Tallacchini 2015.

[H]e saw a rabbit in a cage. It was a white rabbit, with a long, fluffy coat, a pink triangle of a nose, amazed red eyes, ears almost furless flattened against [his] back. [He] wasn't all that big, but in the narrow cage [his] crouching oval body made the wire screen bulge and clumps of fur stuck out, ruffled by a slight trembling. Outside the cage, on the table, there was some grass and the remains of a carrot. Marcovaldo thought of how unhappy the animal must be, shut up in there, seeing that carrot but not being able to eat it. And he opened the door of the cage. The rabbit didn't come out ... Marcovaldo took the carrot and held it closer, then slowly drew it back, to urge the rabbit to come out. The rabbit followed him.

The rabbit is hungry, distressed, restrained, disconnected from his world. He is clearly in a state of constriction, which involves all the aspects listed above. The truly surprising detail in this passage, however, is the animal's hesitation to leave the cage. This conduct – a form of "internalized imprisonment" recognizable in lab animals (Acampora 2006: 99) – mirrors in particular the lack of a "freedom to express (most) normal behavior," which for rabbits would be to dig a hole and flee. Rabbits, indeed, owe their Latin name (*cuniculus*, tunnel) precisely to their tendency to excavate subterranean burrows, which they use to store food, find shelter, reproduce, and give birth.[43] This habit is also associated with their ability to escape from the enclosures where, since the early phases of their domestication, they were kept as "sentient commodities" (Wilkie 2017). What is thwarted here is, therefore, the very "nature" of the rabbit. This makes the rabbit the epitome of all encaged animals that try to retrieve their *natural* (and species-specific *cultural*) liberty – the liberty to exist and have "sufficient space, proper facilities and company of [their] own kind."[44]

In addition to symbolizing confined animals, the rabbit is also the icon of animal testing. A famous example is the campaign against the cosmetic corporation Revlon, promoted by Henry Spira, activist and founder of Animal Rights International. On April 15, 1980, Spira paid the *The New York Times* to publish a full-page picture of an eye-wounded white rabbit and two chemical bottles, bearing the header "How many rabbits does Revlon blind for beauty's sake?" This ad was the first step of a campaign against "extreme ocular toxicity" or "Draize" tests (named after John Draize, who introduced them in 1944): an experiment consisting of applying chemicals to the eyes of animals in order to monitor ocular tissue damage. Spira's campaign was successful, leading to

---

[43] So writes the French historian Robert Delort in his monumental *Les animaux ont une histoire*: "Our western rabbit was baptized by Linnaeus as *Oryctolagus cuniculus*, namely the excavator (*oruktés*) hare (*lagos*) of the kind *connin* [French for *cuniculus*] (hole digger)" (1984: 302, my translation). On the rabbit, see pp. 299–320.

[44] On the evolutionary history of the European rabbit (*Oryctolagus cuniculus*) and its domestication, see Monnerot et al. 1994. See also https://en.wikipedia.org/wiki/European_rabbit.

Revlon's dismissal of these exams. Other cosmetic companies also followed suit, and substantial amounts of money were donated for the development of alternative research. Although moderately, Draize tests are still employed today. As Gary Francione observes,

> albino rabbits are ... used for these tests because their eyes are large, clear, and easily observable, and because the tearing of their eyes, appreciably less than that of other animals' eyes, does not wash away or dilute the substance to be tested. The rabbits are usually restrained in stocks that immobilize their heads and bodies so that they cannot struggle or rub their eyes. Rabbits have been known to break their backs struggling to free themselves from these stocks. The test usually continues for seven days ... After the test is completed, the animals are either killed or recycled into another experiment" (2000: 45).

This detailed description is perfectly consonant with Calvino's picture of the life of the lab rabbit, "forced into a buttoned-up jacket" and exposed to painful experiments. Challenging the "philosophical" stereotype of the "animal as automaton" that has long dominated (and de facto still dominates) science, in *Marcovaldo* as well as in other works, Calvino never questions the nonhuman capacity to suffer. Although this might sound obvious, we must remember that scientific research has begun to prove that animals have mental and emotional lives – "that their actions are purposeful, and that they can indeed suffer" – only since the since the 1950s.[45] By describing Marcovaldo's encounter with the rabbit as based on a common bodily and emotional dimension, Calvino is therefore giving narrative representation to all these conceptual considerations and experimental tests. Throughout the story, the rabbit is depicted as melancholic, depressed, unhappy. However, his experience is not limited to a passive absorption of external stimuli, but mirrors a richer emotional world, wherein the memory of past encounters mingles with hopes, needs, and anticipations. Interactions with others – and notably humans – are an integral part of this world. In one of the final passages, depicting the temporary freedom involuntarily obtained by the bunny, Calvino writes:

> The animal had noticed these lures, these silent offers of food. And though [he] was hungry, [he] didn't trust them. [He] knew that every time humans tried to attract [him] with offers of food, something obscure and painful happened: either they stuck a syringe into [his] flesh, or a scalpel, or they

---

[45] Akhtar 2018: 485. Since the 1950s, experimenters have been carrying out tests proving the capacity of nonhuman animals (from rats to primates) to empathize with other individuals, for example, refusing to accept food by pressing a lever, if this causes another animal in a neighboring cage to receive an electric shock. These experiments also include expressions of joy and pleasure: "Rub a rat's belly, and she or he will emit ultrasonic chirping sounds, believed to have the same neural underpinnings as human laughter" (Akhtar 2018: 485).

forced [him] into a buttoned-up jacket … And the memory of these misfortunes merged with the pain [he] felt inside, with the slow change of organs that [he] sensed, with the prescience of death. And hunger. But as if [he] knew that, of all these discomforts, only hunger could be allayed, and recognized that these treacherous human beings could provide, in addition to cruel sufferings, a sense – which [he] also needed – of protection, of domestic warmth, [he] decided to surrender, to play the humans' game: then whatever had to happen, would happen. (1983b: 58)

In his life of loneliness and pain, of returning motivations and frustrated desires, the rabbit keeps in his body the memory of his relations with people and yet continues to seek them, confirming the complexity of his affective subjectivity. This passage adds yet another common facet to the way humans and nonhuman animals relate to the world. Like Marcovaldo, the rabbit is able to recognize the signs around him. He is clearly a creature capable of reading and interpreting his environment: a semiotic creature. He is able to decipher and make sense of things and behaviors, inferring consequences from them. By stressing the rabbit's bodily memory, need for sympathy, and interpretive ability, Calvino attributes to him intentionality and agency which are squarely at odds with the very "philosophy" of animal tests. Far from being merely anthropomorphic representations, these parallels allude to the deep evolutionary similarities that connect our species to other animal species.[46]

Going back to the larger issue of animal tests, it is important to quote some figures and data. According to *PETA*, "each year, more than 100 million animals – including mice, rats, frogs, dogs, cats, rabbits, hamsters, guinea pigs, monkeys, fish, and birds – are killed in US laboratories for biology lessons, medical training, curiosity-driven experimentation, and chemical, drug, food, and cosmetics testing" (PETA n.d.). In the EU, with similar figures, rodents and rabbits constitute 82.2 percent of the total number.[47] The level of cruelty in laboratories is notorious. Experiments encompass a number of excruciating procedures, many of which are inflicted without anesthesia.[48] In this process, the aliveness and sentience of the imprisoned animals is suppressed. Transformed into data, they are subjected to a "total disembodiment – whereby animal identity is denaturalized to the point of becoming almost immaterial" (Acampora 2006: 102). By approaching the rabbit, recognizing him as a fellow

---

[46] Zoosemiotics and zooanthropology are the two frameworks for this discourse. See Marchesini 2005; Maran 2020; Martinelli 2010.

[47] Knight 2011: 18. Using data for 2007, released by the EU in 2010, Knight reports that the second largest group (9.6 percent) was made up of fish, amphibians, and reptiles, followed by birds (6.4 percent); horses, donkeys, pigs, goats, sheep, and cattle (1.4 percent); and nonhuman primates (0.1 percent). Results are not always reliable, also due to the effects of stress (62–63, 83).

[48] On this, see also Peggs 2018.

sentient being whose corporeal emotions are kin to his, and bringing him home, Marcovaldo re-embodies him in the fullness of his animal identity.

This leads us to the other side of Marcovaldo's "inter-animal" relationship with the rabbit: his plan to turn the animal into a meal. Although apparently contradictory, this plan is perfectly coherent with Marcovaldo's attempts to fetch his own food, almost in the hunter-gatherer spirit. Following Paul Shepard (1998a), one could say that, through all these efforts, Marcovaldo is trying to "come home to the Pleistocene." However, around him the Pleistocene is over, and so is, probably, the Holocene as well. In this new reality, industrialized Capital imposes on "nature" a subjugation system, in which Marcovaldo is also involved, most of the time as a victim. Far from being an abstract "nature-loving" city dweller, in this scenery he is prey and predator. Vis-à-vis the rabbit, Marcovaldo rediscovers in himself the "tender carnivore" (Shepard, again: Shepard 1998b); but, as a subproletarian victim of capitalist exploitation, he is a hungry carnivore. Fallen into the Capitalocene from his preindustrial world, Marcovaldo does not feel the moral need to be a vegetarian. In this dimension of ontological horizontality and visceral, ancestral kinship, seeing a "friendly presence" as food is not a contradiction: "The man stroked [him] on the back and, meanwhile, squeezed it, to see if it was fat. . . . And he looked at [him] with the loving eye of the breeder who manages to allow kindness towards the animal to coexist with anticipation of the roast, all in one emotion" (Calvino 1983: 52).

But there is an extra layer to this discourse. This must be found in Marcovaldo's refusal to accept the industrialization of "nature," and hence the kind of interspecies relationships typical of the Anthropocene. Eating animals whose corporeality is not neutralized into the "mass term *meat*" is an ethical reaction to a production system based on the disconnection of (human) food and (animal) bodies.[49] By being animated by a "nutritional intentionality" toward many of the edible natures he encounters (pigeons, fish, rabbit, mushrooms, etc.), Marcovaldo enacts a subversive strategy against a production system in which food is completely disembodied: there is no longer a connection between the situated life of the animal (or vegetable) that was once a unique being and what is now on our plate – and that finally becomes our body.

Precisely because of this material situatedness in a world in which edible bodies are "variants of my own flesh" (Abram 2010: 192), *Marcovaldo* is never a romantic elegy about a hypothetical Arcadia.[50] Rather, through the

---

[49] Adams 2018: 6. This disconnection is one of the tenets of ecofeminist food studies – and ecofeminism in general. The works of Carol Adams are an epitome of this.

[50] The episode "A Journey with the Cows," in which Marcovaldo's son Michelino "romantically" follows a herd to the mountain pastures and ends up being exploited as an under-age laborer, exemplifies this.

protagonist of this book, Calvino is telling us that every ideology of disembodiment is ipso facto a cognitive, existential, and ethical eclipse. Living in the city can itself become an ideology of disembodiment, if it prevents us from seeing how deeply the city (and our life within it) can depend on "nature." This implies a loss of sensorial capacity, an alienation from the shared sphere of signs on which the cross-species intersubjectivity that shaped our evolution is built. So framed, a "compassionate" and responsible carnivorism plays a role in this intersubjectivity as well as in ecological relationships.[51] In the words of Dominique Lestel (2016), this is "ethical carnivorism": an attitude about eating animals based on the idea that it renews our biological and coevolutionary debt toward its life, and the belief (common, for example, among indigenous people such as the North America Algonquin) that eating animals celebrates their existence, confirming how deeply "human life and death are inextricably bound up with the life and death of other earthly creatures" (Steiner 2016: xiii).

Calvino returned to this topic thirty years later in his final narrative work, *Mr. Palomar* (1983). In an episode titled "Marble and Blood," the protagonist – an older, well-off, pensive, educated, and cosmopolitan version of Marcovaldo – sees in the body of a slaughtered ox both the "person of a disemboweled brother" and the "promise of gustatory happiness" (Calvino 1985: 78). Palomar is well aware that the "quartered carcasses" hanging from the butcher's hooks are there "to remind you that your every morsel is part of a being whose living completeness has been arbitrarily torn asunder" (77), and that our very civilization is not simply human, but based on symbiosis with the animals that we eat. Yet, he participates in this asymmetrical symbiosis with the dilemma that makes civilization itself a long, inexplicable line of abuses and progress. Whereas Marcovaldo situates himself *before the guilt*, Palomar lives this dilemma, feeling that reason cannot solve it, and that it challenges even the most basic logical law, the noncontradiction principle: "One sentiment does not exclude another: Mr. Palomar's mood as he stands in line in the butcher shop is at once of restrained joy and fear, desire and respect, egoistic concern and universal compassion, the mood that perhaps others express in prayer" (78). This coincidence of extremes is also due to the fact that, evolutionarily, we are all flesh variations in the same predation circle, so united "under the same fate" that – as Roberto Marchesini says – "every slaughter is a self-slaughter" (2017: 99).

In *Marcovaldo*, however, the predation system is not closed, and the roles are not interchangeable. As in the beginning, the impersonal institution of the hospital continues to embody the biopower exercised over life. At the end of

---

[51] See Rigby 2020.

the episode, both the rabbit and Marcovaldo (with his family) re-enter the hospital not simply as patients, but as passive prey. In a significant position swap, the rabbit is anthropomorphized: he is described as self-aware and desperate to the point of refusing his own life. On the other hand, Marcovaldo and his family are "lagomorphized" – namely, transformed into rabbits and used as bodies for chemical experiments. Moreover, they are literally "proletarians," reproducing themselves like rabbits. The biopolitical dimension of this episode is totally revealed. The way capitalism and big pharmaceutical corporations use sentient bodies and control life is the gist of this story that dreams about sympathy and companionship between humans and rabbits.

5 The Hen

In the garden of his holiday house, Mr. Palomar listens to the whistling conversations of a couple of blackbirds. Quietly, he and his wife muse on these dialogues taking place in a territory that is at the same time linguistically unbridgeable and yet perfectly within a horizon of meaning. Meditations on the birds' landscape of signs and messages continue when they are back in the city. Here, from his terrace overlooking the "Junoesque" body of Rome, Mr. Palomar observes pigeons and other fowls (Calvino 1985: 55). Every autumn, punctually, flocks of starlings punctuate the sky with their choreographic flights. How does the city appear in the eyes of a bird? This is what Palomar tries to imagine as he reflects about what a phenomenon like the return of starlings means to him. It is the regularity of a pattern, of seasons, of a nature that comes back to claim possession of the sky, even a big city like this. Yet, the elusive mass of birds, moving in shapes that are at once harmonic and explosive, overwhelms him. He's even annoyed by their occupation of the trees along the Tiber. But there is another feeling, perhaps rooted in the cognitive dissonance he experiences as a "civilized" man, sedentary in space and linear in time, vis-à-vis the cyclical return of seasons and birds: "A reassuring sight, the passage of migratory birds is associated in our ancestral memory with the harmonious succession of the seasons; instead, Mr. Palomar feels something akin to apprehension. Can it be because this crowding of the sky reminds us that the balance of nature has been lost?" (62). Probably, this loss is true: the birds "do not fit well in modern human civilization and Palomar, the (high)modern intellectual who is an advanced product of such civilization, cannot understand them, indeed can barely describe what he sees."[52]

Mysterious, disquieting, and immanently semiotic, Palomar's blackbirds, pigeons, and starlings are not the only feathery presences upon which Calvino

---

[52] Bolongaro 2009: 118.

exerts his narrative imagination, every time challenging the boundaries of anthropocentrism. In fact, the bird population, in his works, if not copious in size, is notable in appearance. One of his first animal characters, the hawk Babeuf in *The Path to the Nest of Spiders*, haunts the reader with his mutilated wings and violent death, resonating with the inner world of the protagonist Pin. Also famous is the "municipal pigeon," which is an animal (and an edible one) only in Marcovaldo's eyes, whereas the city council claims it as a solid piece of property. In all these cases, Calvino's birds are both symbols and individuals in flesh and blood: symbols of a world of signs and meanings beyond the human, and individual animals that are often in collision with *our* world of signs and meanings, which is always already a world of power relationships. This is particularly evident when this world materializes in the city, a place where (for Calvino, by definition) "nature" hides, and even more so if it is compelled to do so, crushed by the weight of Anthropocene forces. Pulled out of their environments of life and meanings, animals are often shoved into our sphere of production and consumption, either as food or as workers forced to become unwavering bolts in the machinery of Capital.

One of these animals is the hen that we encounter in a small suburban factory, where other workers – human, this time – are deployed to keep the machine in motion. This happens in "La gallina di reparto" ("The Workshop Hen," 1954), a story wherein the innocence of an apparently "stupid" animal is confronted with the "guilty stupidity" of an oppressive system, in which production justifies abuses and repression across species.[53] Included in the collection *I racconti* (1958), "The Workshop Hen" belongs to a section significantly named "Gli idilli difficili" (Difficult idylls), whose general theme is, in Calvino's words, "the search for and the difficulty in finding a natural harmony, with things and [humans]."[54] Famously, "idyll" is the genre that, since the Greek poet Theocritus, has celebrated natural settings and pastoral life. This title, therefore, perfectly portrays the dissonant relationship between industrial modernity and a residual nature that is here almost unrecognizable, like an archeological inscription that nobody is able (or willing) to decipher. "Difficult Idylls" also includes many of *Marcovaldo*'s episodes, and in fact their world is the same one in which Marcovaldo lives: a dimension wherein freedom and imagination are always frustrated vis-à-vis the "rational, coherent, and practical nonsense" of the industrial universe.[55]

---

[53] The contrast between the "innocently stupid nature" of the hen and the "guilty stupidity" of the oppressive capitalist system is in Ferretti 1989: 43.

[54] Letter to Elio Vittorini, September 5, 1958. Calvino 2013: 165.

[55] Quote from Ferretti 1989: 43. Although its first episodes were written and published already in 1952, *Marcovaldo* appeared as an autonomous volume only in 1963. See Calvino 2003: I, 1366–1389.

The plot is once again in tune with the combination of bittersweet comedy and moral apologue so typical of Calvino's early works. Brought into the factory by a security man called Adalberto, a hen is left free to roam about, searching for earthworms. Sociable and quiet, she regularly lays her eggs, encouraging Adalberto's dream of starting a chicken coop. Soon, however, her "efficiency" sparks a competition among the workers, who attempt all possible tricks to gain her favor – and hence her "production." The clumsy traffics around the bird arouse the suspicions of the factory's heads, which are also fomented by an envious whistleblower. Alleged to be the vehicle – through her ovary duct – of messages about a union strike, the hen is first carefully (and painfully) inspected, then sentenced to death. The story ends with her execution in the "dingy courtyard" of the factory: so silent in life, the stupefied creature throws now "a last long heart-breaking shriek, then a lugubrious cluck." Adalberto's dream of a chicken coop is eventually shattered, and so is the precarious coexistence of factory and farm, ultimately erased by the new industrial order and its perverse mechanisms. Meanwhile, in the background, a real union revolt is about to rise, completely unrelated to the hen and the suspected workers. Its effects will reverberate up through some higher rungs of the factory's hierarchy, as we read in the final scene: "Thus does the machine of oppression ever turn against those who serve it."[56]

Despite its prima facie simplicity, this story invites a plurality of interpretive layers. A Marxist reading is almost obvious: considering its historical frame and specific topic, "The Workshop Hen" is a working-class story, written while Calvino was still affiliated with the Italian Communist Party (PCI), from which he would distance himself only three years later. With its emphasis on the industrial exploitation and transformation of matter and life, this reading aligns distinctly with the Anthropocene or – even more – the Capitalocene. However, if we use the environmental humanities toolbox, more layers come to the surface, and "The Workshop Hen" becomes a story about a mutating landscape, a disappearing environment of signs for multispecies relationships, and even an invisible wave of extinction.

The Marxist background of the narration is easy to pinpoint. In fact, "The Workshop Hen" belongs to a creative cluster that, between 1950 and 1954, Calvino was planning to dedicate to life in an industrial city. This project also included the fragments of two novels, *I giovani del Po* ("The Po river youth") and *La collana della regina* ("The queen's necklace"). "The Hen" was initially conceived as a chapter of the latter before it ended up in the "Difficult Idylls." Through these stories, Calvino aimed at orienting his literary production around

---

[56] Quotes in Calvino 1995: 78.

a social-realist nucleus: "I wanted to express in a narrative form ... the city, the industrial civilization, and workers; and, along with that, that part of reality and of my interests ... that is nature, adventure, and the difficult pursuit of a natural happiness today," he wrote in a note of 1957 (2003: III, 1342). The cluster was not a successful experiment, though: most of its segments remained unfinished or unpublished.[57] Yet, this seeming "failure" shows how labels are often unable to contain the multitudes of literary creativity, and indeed Calvino's stories enrich "working-class literature" with an unprecedented density of motives, going well beyond this genre's canons, especially when it comes to illuminating the problematic relationship between "nature" and happiness against the backdrop of mechanized labor. In "The Workshop Hen," this density is concentrated in the parallel representation of the bird and the workers, whose lives and worlds are both trapped in the pens of "industrial civilization."

Calvino adopts a stylistic strategy through which the bond between hen and workers and the violence of the systems are progressively revealed, resulting in a final conflict that is embodied by the factory itself. Everything starts with the setting, which at first appears nearly bucolic. The factory is evidently built on the scraps of a rural territory, and the hen is allowed to leave her cage during the day and enjoy a kind of "freedom and irresponsibility," for which workers envy her. Yet, in this limbo, she is a worker, too: she is "a good layer" (1995: 70) whose function, exactly like everyone else's in the factory, is to produce ("at least one egg a day": 70). Like her human "colleagues," she also is exploited and alienated from her own production. Unlike them, however, she is the ideal worker, "a quiet creature who would never dare upset the severe industrial atmosphere" (70). In this space of silenced freedom, while the hen is somehow humanized, the (other) workers resemble hybrids between "extensions of the machine" (Marx's famous expression) and "trained gorillas" – a metaphor attributed to Frederick Taylor, that Calvino had certainly encountered in Antonio Gramsci's *Prison Notebooks*.[58] In their "mechanized animality," the only freedom on which workers can rely is to maintain the flux of their thoughts as they operate on the assembly line. In one passage, for example, we read:

> For eight hours a day, Pietro rotated round the four machines making the same series of movements every time, movements he knew so well now he had managed to shave off every superfluous blip and adjust the rhythm of his

---

[57] On this cluster, see Scarpa 1999: 214–216.

[58] For Frederick Taylor, eponymous of "Taylorism," and his notion of the manual worker as a "trained gorilla," see Gramsci's "Americanism and Fordism" (*Notebook* 4, § 52), in Gramsci 1977: 277–318. It is interesting to note that the original title of Gramsci's manuscript was "'Animality' and Industrialism" (see Gramsci 1977: 489). For an analysis of this metaphor in "The Workshop Hen," see Carnemolla 2019: 175–176.

asthma to that of his work with perfect precision. Even his eyes moved along trajectories as precise as the stars ... But so inexhaustible a quality is man's freedom, that even in these conditions Pietro's mind was able to weave its web from one machine to the other, ... and in the midst of this geometry of steps gestures glances and reflexes he would sometimes find he was master of himself once again and calm as a country grandfather going out late in the morning to sit under the pergola and stare at the sun and whistle for his dog and keep an eye on his grandchildren swinging on a tree and watch the figs ripen day by day. (Calvino 1995: 72)

Keeping hints of "nature" alive, as Marcovaldo also tries to do, can be for these workers an ultimately subversive gesture, a stubborn form of resistance. And here, too, as in *Marcovaldo*, it is patent that certain humans, just like other nondominant animal species, are themselves victims of the hegemonic pathways of the capitalist Anthropocene. This is brought to an extreme in the tale's final scene, in which the factory qua capital seems to prevail even over the workshop's heads. One can therefore say conclusively that "The Workshop Hen" is a Capitalocene story.[59] In fact, even more openly than in other narratives, here the organization of human and nonhuman life is a result of the inextricable relations of "capital, power, and nature as an organic whole."[60] Its driving mechanism is a system of production and accumulation that thrives on the creation of "Cheap Nature," to use Jason Moore's expression. And Marxism is, as already mentioned, a privileged political and cultural horizon for Calvino. Yet, as the fate of the planned narrative cluster and the trans-species angle of the hen's story demonstrate, it would be reductive to encase Calvino's creativity – and even his being a communist – within a political orthodoxy. In fact, the kind of communism Calvino was embracing in those years was a somewhat heretical, anarchic, and even liberal communism, refractory to ideological rigors, and more indebted to "the example of the communists in flesh-and-blood" that he had encountered during the Resistance than to "the classics of Marxism-Leninism." Perhaps for this reason a fellow partisan and journalist, Paolo Spriano, described him as "the most joyful and least problematic communist I have ever met," someone who "wanted to do just anything, the

---

[59] I thank Cristina Carnemolla (2019) for developing this reflection in my graduate seminar on Calvino and the Anthropocene. Her article provides an interesting interpretation of "The Workshop Hen" in connection to these issues.

[60] Moore 2016b: 81. Capitalism, explains Moore, "is a world-ecology that joins the accumulation of capital, the pursuit of power, and the co-production of nature in successive historical configurations" (Moore 2016b: 7). On "Cheap Nature," Moore writes (2016b: 2): "For capitalism, Nature is 'cheap' in a double sense: to make Nature's elements 'cheap' in price; and also *to cheapen*, to degrade or to render inferior in an ethico-political sense, the better to make Nature cheap in price." See also Moore 2015.

revolutionary and the writer, the editor and the journalist."[61] Calvino would be a supporter of the Left throughout his entire life. However, it does not come as a surprise that in 1957 he parted ways with the PCI because it had backed the USSR's armed suppression of the Hungarian revolution in 1956. The point is that, although his working-class sympathies were deep and sincere, his vision was simply larger, prone to a more "humane" and even postanthropocentric Marxism, that would embrace humans, animals, and the landscape in a single view.

And the landscape is the next focus of our interpretation of "The Workshop Hen." Conceived in the bloom of the post-World War II industrialization, the story distinctly mirrors its identity shift from the rural to the industrial as fast-paced development collapsed the physical boundaries between these two dimensions. The Italian territory bears eloquent signs of this "Great Transformation," which in many cases openly coincides with the "Great Acceleration" of the Anthropocene.[62] These are the years in which Calvino himself would describe the tentacular urban expansion and the pervasiveness of industrial pollution not only in *Marcovaldo*, but also in his short novel *Smog* (1958), which delineates the rising contamination that infiltrates everything in the city, from bodies to information. Rampant building speculation and its assault upon the traditional landscape are also addressed in another novella, *A Plunge into Real Estate* (1957), in which the harmonious natural–cultural features of his native region literally crumble alongside the political ideals of the Resistance.[63]

Other important writers have also put this topic at center stage. For example, Pier Paolo Pasolini (2014) describes the post-World War II modernization of Rome in his famous poem "The Cry of the Excavator" (1957), denouncing a mutant landscape that is also the backdrop of his novels (*The Ragazzi*, 1955; *A Violent Life*, 1959) and films (*Accattone*, 1961; *Mamma Roma*, 1962). Also in 1957, the "industrial" novelist Ottiero Ottieri pictures the evolution of the Milanese rural outskirts in his book *Tempi stretti* ("Tight times") with these words: "Advancing, the city has incorporated entire agricultural villages with farmhouses and churches adorned with a bell tower. . . . The factories were born from the fields, from the earth; but the destroyed countryside, as weak and pale as the sky, does not seem to defend itself, and no one regrets it" (2001: 20).

---

[61] Quotes (including Spriano's words) in Scarpa 1999: 207–208.

[62] I am following here the landscape anthropologist and semiologist Eugenio Turri, especially in his *Semiologia del paesaggio italiano* (1990). On the "Great Transformation" of the Italian landscape in the 1960s–70s, see Turri 1990: 3–27 and *passim*. See also Settis 2012 and Vallerani 2013.

[63] *Smog* and *A Plunge into Real Estate*, along with *The Argentine Ant*, are also part of the *Racconti*, in the section "La vita difficile" ("Difficult life").

Similarly, Alberto Moravia, Anna Maria Ortese, Giorgio Bassani, Carlo Cassola, and Giorgio Caproni also voice the "slow apocalypse" of the country through their works.

Living and working in Turin, with Milan and Genoa as the other points of Italy's industrial triangle, Calvino experienced this changing landscape first-hand. In fact, especially in the more developed North, the small and medium-sized workshops still coexisted, in those years, with large factories as well as with agricultural farms. It was almost an evolutionary territory in which the signs of the past were still inscribed beneath the new functional forms, making the transformation legible in its various stages.[64] This is precisely the setting of "The Workshop Hen." Beyond its programmatic quality of "working-class tale," this story mirrors, therefore, an epochal zoo-anthropological mutation, representing the ultimate alienation of the Holocene signs in the new Anthropocene landscape.

The space of the factory, for example, is a formerly rural ground caught by Calvino in the very moment of becoming industrial. The first piece of evidence comes from the courtyard, which had been "only recently annexed to the purposes of industry," and therefore "abounded not only in rusty screws but likewise in worms." And here comes yet another layer of our reading, this time elicited by adopting a multispecies ethnography and biosemiotic lens. On this transient territory, in fact, there is also something which directly touches the relationship of the hen with her surrounding humans. "Tame as a cat by nature" and "on friendly terms" with the workers to the point that she "let herself be picked up" and "prodded under the tail," the hen is halfway between a companion animal and livestock.[65] She is a source of food and, at the same time, she is clearly depicted as a subject with an emotional life: not only *zoë*, but *bios* as well. Indeed, chickens – animals proven to be "on par with many mammals in terms of their level of intelligence, emotional sophistication, and social interaction" and whose domestication is thought to have occurred in the first phases of the Holocene – belong by all means to a companion species.[66]

However, in a context in which the signs and messages of a rural past are losing their meanings, this relational density is no longer understandable. The German–Estonian zoologist Jakob von Uexküll has defined *Umwelt*, or semiotic environment, the web of marks and significant carriers of information in which every species is immersed and whose interpretation is key to life itself. An

---

[64] On Calvino's mutating landscapes, see Seger 2015: 24–49, and Iovino 2018.

[65] Quotes in Calvino 1995: 70; 74; 76.

[66] Marino 2017: 127. On chicken domestication, see Tixier-Boichard et al. 2011; Miao et al. 2013; and Peters et al. 2015. On the controversial issue of the origins of domestic chickens, see Wang et al. 2020.

Umwelt is a space that materially oozes with the signs and meanings indispensable for living beings not only to survive, but to be alive at all. These semiotic environments are species-specific, but not closed: they intersect, forming a common semiosphere, which allows for interspecies communication and experience.[67] Now, with the transitions of workers and their sphere of signs from the farm to the factory, the *Umwelt* of chickens and that of their human cohabitants no longer overlap. The ties of species companionship slowly dissolve, determining the impossibility to continue a coexistence that was a Holocene form of cooperation, a coworking. Coworking is not meant to be a romanticization here. In fact, as the French sociologist Jocelyne Porcher suggests (in collaboration with philosopher Vinciane Despret), exploitation in pastoralist societies is not the only possible interspecies relational schema. There are invisible forms of cooperation between farm animals and farmers that have developed on the basis of their intersecting semiospheres over millennia. Unlike the mechanical violence that underlies the "production-at-any-cost" model, in this relation animals "implicate themselves, give, exchange, receive, and because it is not exploitative, farmers give, receive, exchange, and grow along with their animals" (Despret 2016: 178).

In this context, nonhuman animals are not necessarily victims and humans not necessarily oppressors, but coevolutionary partners, companion species. Their mutual relationship, as Donna Haraway has taught us, defines them *ex novo*: "the partners do not precede their relating: all that is, is the fruit of becoming with" – a "becoming with" whose "generative connotations [are] always ready to erupt" (2008, 17). This is how Porcher, herself an experienced goat farmer, articulates such a concept: "Work was the place of our unexpected meeting, the possibility of our communication, when we belonged to different species who, before the Neolithic, even before Neanderthals, apparently had nothing to say and nothing to do with one another."[68] This mutually generative conversation began on the ground of shared and intersecting environments of meanings. In a way, these reflections suggest that another form of work outside the factory is possible. The Holocene is sending the Capitalocene a subversive message.

On the other hand, the Capitalocene factory is also itself a system of signs, a semiosphere. The only language and the only signs that the factory recognizes

---

[67] First elaborated by Uexküll (2010 [1934]), the concept of *Umwelt* was developed by Hungarian–American semiotician Thomas Sebeok and also used by Martin Heidegger. It is one of the cornerstones of biosemiotics; namely, "the study of qualitative semiotic processes that are considered to exist in a variety of forms down to the simplest living organisms and to the lowest levels of biological organization" (Maran 2015: 29). On biosemiotics and ecosemiotics, see Maran 2020.

[68] Porcher 2011 quoted in Despret 2016, 183.

are those of efficiency: in this environment, life (human as well as nonhuman) is readable as an instrument of production, an extension of the machine, a cog in the engine of oppression. A hen, "free" and "irresponsible," whose only occupations are to feed on the worms she can find among the rusty screws, sleep, and lay her daily egg, is here a semiotic intruder. She is both a vestigial trait and a syntactic error. Like the caudal vertebrae in the human skeleton, she is an archeological piece of biology lacking any real function. And, like a syntactic error, she is an element out of place, meaningless and unlocalizable in the new discursive order. Her death is therefore also the logical result of a misunderstanding of her as a sign, because she is mistakenly inserted into another story, in which other signs and messages are more predictably exchanged. Completely unaware and materially innocent, she becomes one of these messages, thus mirroring all the ambiguities and antagonisms at play in the factory. Translated into the language of the factory conflicts, which everybody but she understands, the hen becomes an alleged sign vessel in a world of equivocal messages. In this world, she is turned into a sacrificial object: a scapegoat for class conflicts and for the fading clash between the rural and the urban dimension. Still coexisting for the moment, these two spheres are definitely growing apart. The hen is killed because she belongs to a system of signs that the factory is no longer able to decipher. And here Pasolini's verses come to mind: "Death lies not / in not being able to communicate / but in no longer being understood" (2014: 333).

Calvino's story stops there, but it is clear that, in the world where his "Workshop Hen" is historically set, there are already other factories and other chickens. In a surprising coincidence, industrial chicken farming had started in Delaware in 1923, the same year Calvino was born. Italy was closely following this modernization process, which was already emerging in the mid-1920s and reached its completion at the end of the 1950s.[69] From that point on, the only way hens could enter a factory would be as workers (laying hens) or as products (broiler chickens). In both cases, the biopolitical dimension of this oppression would be absolute.

---

[69] See National Chicken Council [n.d.]. On this see also Weis 2013: 73: "In the 1920s, in the Delmarva Peninsula of the eastern USA (Delaware–Maryland–Virginia), an accidental experiment in rearing thousands of chickens in a small space using concentrated feed set off a wave of innovations in warehouses, hatcheries, artificial incubators, feed regimes, and debeaking machines over the next few decades, which involved the rise of some soon-to-be corporate giants like Perdue and Tyson. This take-off was famously signaled by Herbert Hoover's promise during the 1928 presidential election campaign to put 'a chicken in every pot and a car in every garage,' and 'by the start of the 21st century the average American consumed 100 times more chicken than at the start of the 1930s.'" On the development of Italian aviculture, considered from an historical angle, see Trevisani 1902 and 1924; Chigi 1968.

Here we can take our final interpretive step. "The Workshop Hen" is, in its own way, an extinction story. As extinction studies scholars, anthropologists, and philosophers extensively engaged with mass death in the animal realm have made clear, extinction is not an event, but a process – a long wave shattering an entire world of relationships rather than simply "the brute material presence or absence of the animal's body and genetic material" (Wolfe 2017: xi). This process is punctuated by what Deborah Bird Rose calls "deathzones": places where you can still see individuals, but where their worlds are slowly dissolving. In these deathzones "the living and the dying encounter each other in the presence of that which cannot be averted. Death is imminent but has not yet arrived" (Rose 2013: 3–4). Wherever a change occurs in an ecosystem, whenever a culture dies off, along with its entire horizon of meanings, a whole set of creatures also slowly die – and this death does not need to be spectacular or tragic: it simply happens. Yet, death for chickens is hardly undramatic or unrecognizable. And their life is tragic, too. As Tony Weis writes in his *Ecological Hoofprint*, these animals are completely deprived of their agency, their family bonds, their connection with the biological substratum of existence: "In industrial hatcheries, specialized breeder flocks never see their young, as eggs are artificially incubated, hatched, and chicks sold off to growers in large bundles (with the exception of male layer chicks, which are promptly destroyed)" (2013: 96) Industrially raised chickens live all their "lives" in a deathzone, which is the prodrome of all extinction, both existential and biological.

Of course, speaking today of the extinction of chickens sounds like a joke. However, things are not exactly so clear-cut, and for two reasons. The first is the real impact that industrial farming has on the variety of breeds. The FAO's Global Databank for Farm Animal and Genetic Resources reports that, due to the increasing uniformity introduced by "enhanced breeding," out of 7,600 livestock breeds, 190 have become extinct and 1,500 are endangered. In the case of chickens, the specialization into egg "layers" and meat "broilers" has determined a significant decline of less specialized breeds (Weis 2013: 95–96). But there is another, more profound reason for this discourse. Extinction, in fact, is not simply about gene pools; it is also about an entire world of coexistences and of evolutionary coconstructions, it is a "generative conversation" that disappears from history. Considered in this perspective, the masses of broiler or layer chickens, bereft of their ecology of relations, deprived of a real habitat that would necessarily involve a relation with other species, are already extinct. Even though they appear near to innumerable, these chickens resemble the last living representatives of a species that will not survive, like David Quammen's last dodo, that closed her eyes sometime in 1667, unseen, in a corner of a land we call Australia (Quammen 1996: 275).

"The world dies from each absence," wrote Vinciane Despret in her memorable pages on Martha and George, the last couple of passenger pigeons on display in the Cincinnati Zoo, already extinct as a species even before they would cease to exist as individuals, on September 1, 1914. This extinction reverberates from the individual critters to the whole fabric of the universe:

> The world dies from each absence; the world bursts from absence. For . . . the entire universe thinks and feels itself, and each being matters in the fabric of its sensations. Every sensation of every being of the world is a mode through which the world lives and feels itself, and through which it exists. . . . When a being is no more, the world narrows all of a sudden, and a part of reality collapses. Each time an existence disappears, it is a piece of the universe of sensations that fades away. (2017: 219–220)

In Calvino's story, too, to become extinct is, irremediably, a whole world of signs. Deprived of their ecological connections, of their capacity to transform and be transformed by interaction with other species – and to do so physically, cognitively, and emotionally – industrially raised chickens are already extinct. The hen, in her delicate singularity, is just another figure of the dodo. And extinct too is the biocultural landscape, in which hens were free to scratch, and humans free to have dreams about chicken coops, even in a factory.

The final paradox is that, as this Holocene world disappears, the extent of chicken mass-production has become itself epochal, especially if we take seriously the Anthropocene Working Group's implication that "the fossilized bones of trillions of broiler chickens will probably compose a distinctive fossil layer, a proxy for the 'Great Acceleration'" (Farmer 2017: 173). Not animal fossils, but the fossilized remains of mass-produced animal bodies: this is also one of the marks of the Anthropocene's Golden Spike. And here a reflection about the names given to this alleged epoch would be interesting. Like in a shadow play, "Anthropocene" reveals the silhouette of its maker, *Anthropos*. "Capitalocene" in turn gives *Anthropos* a name and a face, shedding light on the framework of its action, Capitalism. But perhaps "Avicene," the Age of Chicken, wouldn't be an inaccurate definition for these composite strata, where the bones of a hoard of different "layers" are turned into the inculpable signs of the geology of the human.

6 The Gorilla

Living otherness on display. This is the zoo. A silent observer, always bewildered by the unpredictable forms of reality, Mr. Palomar wanders along cages and glasshouses, where enclosed creatures seem to him at once kin and radically alien. Giraffes, penguins, reptiles, apes: they are brotherly for their pain, their loneliness, the stridor of their anguished presence, which resonates with his incapacity to find "patterns of harmony" in himself and what he sees. Yet, these animals are alien. Alien are their original habitats, the remote regions from which they or their ancestors were forcibly subtracted. And alien are their inner worlds, which are inaccessible and lost, reduced to an accident of a museified alterity. In fact, subjugated to reinforce the fantasy of human exceptionalism, these creatures disquietingly demonstrate just the opposite, namely that "[b]eyond the glass of every cage, there is the world as it was before man, or as it will be, to show that the world of man is not eternal and is not unique" (Calvino 1985: 86). In the "complicated harmony" of giraffes – graceful despite the apparent gracelessness of their moves – and the "monstrosity, and necessity, and beauty" of reptiles constrained in "a motionless mixture of days and nights" (86), Mr. Palomar sees therefore the manifestation of "an innocent and suffering otherness, a distressing and inscrutable area towards which no self-sufficient exercise of reason is possible or permitted" (Ferretti 1989: 151). All these feelings – of discomfort, sympathy, anxiety, sadness, disorientation – converge vis-à-vis the albino gorilla he sees in Barcelona's Zoo.

To better understand this encounter, we must first consider the nature of *Mr. Palomar*, which is the last volume of fiction Calvino published during his life. "Fiction" is only partially accurate in this case. Written between 1975 and 1983, this is "the most autobiographical book I have ever written, a third-person autobiography," he declared in an interview.[70] Even more poignantly, another writer, Daniele Del Giudice, has defined the character Mr. Palomar as "a middle point, halfway between the first and the third person."[71] Although occasionally present, and certainly sublimated in the shape of landscapes and atmospheres, autobiography is not a constant feature in Calvino's writing. Yet this work, which is an exercise in leaving the self aside or letting it disappear in the mystery of its objects, bears traces of his life and experiences – of his cities and places, his travels, his tastes, his family, even his individual traits.

Looked at more closely, the name *Palomar* has a double referent: a famous telescope in California and a dovecote. Observation and the (frustrated) quest for an order by which to "pigeonhole" phenomena give unity and direction to these twenty-seven episodes, which travel along three experiential paths – description, chronicle, and meditation – and gather into three sections: "Mr. Palomar's Vacation," "Mr. Palomar in the City," and "The Silences of

---

[70] "L'occhio e il silenzio," Interview with Lietta Tornabuoni, *La Stampa*, November 25, 1983: 3, in Calvino 2012: 552.

[71] Quoted in Scarpa 1999: 205.

Mr. Palomar." Mediated through the filter of this persona-observatory and certainly not exhaustive of the author's creative and existential universe, a "Calvino-shadow" emerges in these stories of a taciturn man who lives between Rome, Paris, and the Tyrrhenian sea. From there, he monitors the things that surround him, interrogating himself about their meanings, taxonomies, and kinships, and often caught in smaller or bigger frictions with reality. As Domenico Scarpa has written,

> The most touching aspect of Mr. Palomar is the contradiction in which he lives: he would like to give voice and order to the world, from nocturnal constellations to the grass of his meadow and the cheeses of a Parisian shop, but at the same time he would like to refrain from perturbing it: from upsetting the disharmony of the world by which he feels upset.[72]

Animals often appear in *Mr. Palomar*. We have already met the starlings flying above his terrace and the ox in the butcher shop, but Mr. Palomar's days are filled with nonhuman presences: black birds, turtles, geckoes . . . All of them disclose an abyss and a disappointment: an abyss of mystery about their world of meanings, and a disappointment with his efforts to categorize what he sees. His most challenging experiences, however, occur during his three visits to zoos. The first and the last of these, which happen in France at the Vincennes zoo and Paris' Jardin des Plantes respectively – fall halfway between the aesthetic and the taxonomic. Alone or with his daughter, Palomar observes giraffes and reptiles, contemplating the fraternal "monstrosity" of these captive animals. He tries to locate the place of the human in relation to the "antediluvian bestiary" (Calvino 1983: 87) of which zoo pythons, boas, iguanas, and crocodiles are dismal specimens. But it is the central episode, dedicated to the albino gorilla in Barcelona's zoo, that fully reveals the thickness of the layers – ethical, political, anthropological, and semiotic – that lie behind these cages.[73]

Completely eventless, the plot of "The Albino Gorilla" is built upon the emotional and symbolic density of a meeting. Visiting the primate section, Palomar lingers on Copito de Nieve (Floquet de Neu, in Catalan), a.k.a. Snowflake, a world-famous white gorilla who is one of the zoo's main attractions. And what he finds is a rather depressing – yet thought-provoking – spectacle:

> Beyond a sheet of plate glass, "Copito de Nieve" . . . is a mountain of flesh and white hide. . . . The facial mask is a human pink, carved by wrinkles . . . Every now and then that . . . sad giant . . . turns upon the crowd of visitors beyond the glass . . . a slow gaze charged with desolation and patience and boredom,

---

[72] Scarpa 1999: 206. For *Mr. Palomar*'s three experiential paths, see p. 204.

[73] Quotes in Calvino 1985: 87. On *Mr. Palomar*'s zoo animals, see Rohman 2009.

a gaze that expresses all the resignation at being the way he is, sole exemplar in the world of a form not chosen, not loved, all the effort of bearing his own singularity, and the suffering at occupying space and time with his presence so cumbersome and evident. (Calvino 1985: 81)

In the "enormous void of his hours," the gorilla spends his time hugging a car tire. In this space without nature, without games, without a world, surrounded by a ghastly silence, Mr. Palomar perceives the gorilla as kin, sharing a dimension of solitude, incommunicability, and the need for meanings.

Already very rich in its rarefied poetic intensity, "The Albino Gorilla" acquires added depth if considered in its compositional development. Before re-elaborating this episode as a *Mr. Palomar* chapter, Calvino published it as a short autobiographical feature titled "Visita a un gorilla albino" ("Visiting an Albino Gorilla") in the newspaper *La Repubblica* on May 16, 1980. Speaking in the first person, he provided a slightly more detailed description of Copito de Nieve's life conditions, mentioning, for example, the many attempts at repro-ducing his unique genetic material (something to which we will return later), and observing that the source of the sympathy he felt was due to an "interior situation, also in relationship to the environment, which is completely human, filled with negative human meanings" (Calvino 1980). He also stressed the "prison- and concentration-camp-like aspect" of the gorilla's stall, creating an explicit parallel between zoos and these two extreme confinement institutions. The most remarkable difference with the final version, however, is the presence of an occasional interlocutor, the Uruguayan writer and political exile Juan Carlos Onetti (indicated as "J.C.O."), with whom Calvino shared the story of the gorilla. The writer's comments and Calvino's unspoken answer, omitted in the end, are worth a mention:

> "There's nothing strange about a caged monkey," says O. "I know a man who's been locked up in a much smaller cage for years." . . . I understand that he wanted to give me a lesson in civil morality: one does not speak of the suffering of a caged monkey to the citizen of a country where so many people are imprisoned and tortured.[74]

In the final version, which omits J.C.O., the only thing that captures Mr. Palomar's attention is the inhumane condition in which the gorilla is kept: a state of boredom and placelessness, a semiotic desert. By defining this condition as "inhumane" – an adjective that Calvino does not use – I am not

---

[74] Calvino 1980. Excerpts of this article are in Calvino 2003: II, 1430. As zoologists know well, and as Frans de Waal repeatedly stresses, "monkeys" and "apes" are not the same. In Italian, the word "scimmia," however, roughly translates both terms ("apes" would be "grandi scimmie"). I have chosen to translate "una scimmia in gabbia" as "caged *monkey*" to convey the feeling of nuisance emerging from J.C.O.'s answer.

implying that the gorilla is or should be humanized, but that his situation of total withdrawal from a world of meanings, so understandable for a human being, is indeed the most radical form of inflicted pain for other animals, too. And Calvino, who maintained the heuristic usefulness of anthropomorphism to shed light on ethical and ontological similarities across the species, was well aware of this.[75]

Accordingly, we can see that Mr. Palomar's encounter with the gorilla is indeed an encounter between two environments, both semiotic and material. Mr. Palomar's semiosphere is made up of places and people, objects and things. It is a sedimented human – urban, cosmopolitan, natural–cultural – environment. The signs that he finds and exchanges in this environment are those that allow him to transform his life into a sequence of meaningful experiences, to make sense of conventions like words and books, symbols and institutions, including the cages of a zoo, and the zoo itself. This environment also entails, of course, his biological environment, his species-specific *Umwelt*, and the subterranean lineage that connects him to his evolutionary relatives: Mr. Palomar, too, is a primate. Although uneasy and discomforted, he is free to use his environment, to delve into it, and inhabit it, transforming it into new signs, meanings, descriptions, stories, philosophical reflections. On the other hand, Copito de Nieve's specific *Umwelt* clashes in the zoo with a surrogate environment pervaded by signs and things that do not belong to him or to his species. Confined in a mock garden with only a "squat leafless tree and an iron ladder" (Calvino 1985: 82), the gorilla expresses with his desolated mien "all the effort of bearing his own singularity" (81).

"One can take the ape out of the jungle, but not the jungle out of the ape," writes the primatologist Frans de Waal (2006: 1). Disentangled from the jungle and its living stories, Copito de Nieve lives suspended in an uncanny void. Now that the signs of his original *Umwelt* are blurred and lost, he spends indefinite spans of time relating to a tire – and this tire, Mr. Palomar infers, becomes in his hands something else: "What can this object be for him? A toy? A fetish? A talisman?" (1985: 82). For a moment, Mr. Palomar puts forward the hypothesis that the tire is an emotional medium, a symbol that helps the gorilla hold onto reality. The tire, one may assume, could be a symbol of Copito's solitude, of his difficult singularity, of his alienated presence in a world poor of signs intelligible to him. But these are only arbitrary interpretations. It would be more accurate to say, as a tour guide does, upon whom Mr. Palomar eavesdrops in Mexico by the ruins of Tula, that we don't know what it means: *"No se sabe lo qué quiere decir"* (97). What is clear, in the intersection of their two sign-universes, is the need that both Mr. Palomar and

---

[75] On a reappraisal of anthropomorphism in evaluating the primates' emotions, see de Waal 2018.

Copito de Nieve have of "investing oneself in things, recognizing oneself in signs, transforming the world into a collection of symbols – a first daybreak of culture in the long biological night" (83).

Now, that might sound – and perhaps is – an excessively anthropomorphic interpretation. However, the shared need for meaningful signs is a very significant aspect here. Indeed, the evolutionary connections between humans and nonhumans – especially mammals and primates – underpin the innumerable parallels in the ways different species relate to the world and their members in terms of experience, sociability, conflict, emotions, communication, and feelings. These parallels are evident and yet for a long time have been largely underestimated. Consider how powerfully the "Cartesian scientific practice" of classical behaviorism, with its "rigidly disciplined experimental regimes in controlled laboratory settings" (Westling 2016: 28–29) has confined animals, even those historically and biologically closer to our species, to a limbo of nonmind. In contrast, the so-called "bi-constructivist paradigm" associated with multispecies ethnography, anthrozoology, modern primatology, zoosemiotics, and the cognitive and phenomenological strands of ethology, "takes as axiomatic the subjectivity of animals," considering humans not as mere observers, but as partners in a mutual construction of worlds and experiences (Lestel et al. 2014: 127). This means that human/animal relationships are intrinsically intersubjective, and that they are, therefore, cognitively and semiotically charged. Many scientists and primatologists, whose names also appear in these pages, have helped to rehabilitate the qualitative dimension of nonhuman intelligence and emotional worlds, showing that, if we work *with* animals rather than working *on* them, a whole universe of similarities emerges. And this is a semiotic universe, a universe of signs. This universe is what defines the "hybrid communities" that humans form with nonhumans in society as "semiotic communities" (Lestel 2002: 55). The nonhuman semiosphere intersects that of the human observer (or better: partner in action), shaping an actively storied dimension that brings together subjects, places, and their shared becoming. Exploring these similarities from the viewpoint of the primates' emotions, Frans de Waal insists that "Our species shares many emotions with the other primates because we rely on approximately the same behavioral repertoire. This similarity, expressed by bodies with similar design, gives us a profound nonverbal connection with other primates. Our bodies map so perfectly onto theirs, and vice versa, that mutual understanding is close behind" (2019: 19–20). It is for this reason that Calvino's description of the gorilla's boredom, his solitude and need for semiotic fulfillment, is so anthropomorphic and yet so realistic – and so accurate. Mr. Palomar and Copito de Nieve are both singularly involved in a semiotic dimension. This analogy was already evident in the episode of the

"Poisonous Rabbit," where Marcovaldo and the rabbit could both "interpret" a cage, a carrot, even a surgical tool. It is true that, as defined by Uexküll (2010 [1934]), *Umwelten* are species-specific world-contexts, environments of signs in which all organisms are immersed, just as they are immersed in a physical context. However, this "immersion is not only sensorial but based on motivations, emotions, knowledge, specific cognitive functions. We are mistaken when we say that different *Umwelten* are separated, because they overlap: there are wide areas of sharing between species" (Marchesini 2017: 15).

The problem here is that this dimension is not a "semiotic community" in Lestel's terms. Between their intersecting environments of signs, there is a one-way form of relation, a frustrated intersubjectivity, which is embodied by the nonmutual gaze that Mr. Palomar throws at the gorilla. The confined framework of the zoo makes any real encounter impossible. As John Berger wrote in his seminal 1977 essay "Why Look at Animals?," any connection between humans and nonhuman animals in the zoo is thwarted. Created in an epoch in which animals were disappearing from the sphere of everyday experience, the zoo "to which people go to meet animals, to observe them, to see them, is, in fact, a monument to the impossibility of such encounters."[76] In the zoo, animals are marginalized both culturally and physically, and this marginality is not only, Berger continued, connected to the general disappearance of animals – what we now call the "Sixth Extinction." Instead, it is linked to breaking the reciprocity of the gaze between human and animal:

> nowhere in a zoo can a stranger encounter the look of an animal. At the most, the animal's gaze flickers and passes on. . . . Therein lies the ultimate consequence of their marginalization. That look between animal and man, which may have played a crucial role in the development of human society, . . . has been extinguished. . . . This historic loss, to which zoos are a monument, is now irredeemable for the culture of capitalism (1980: 26).

This loss also entails the very density of the presence of the animal as a sentient, carnal, living being. Especially in a postmodern culture in which the dominating medium is the image (and this is the culture to which Calvino relates in these years), the animals in flesh and blood are reduced to phantasms, abstract figures whose "frailties and stress" vanish "along with our sympathy" (Spotte 2006: 15). Neither John Berger nor Calvino could know, but this epoch of "historic loss" is what we now call the Anthropocene.

This consideration takes us to another aspect of this story that has both an individual side, totally embodied by the singular persona of Copito de Nieve,

---

[76] Berger 1980: 21. Although there is no concrete proof for this, it is not impossible that Calvino had read Berger's essay. On Calvino's "gaze," see Belpoliti 2006.

and a larger historical narrative. The story of Copito de Nieve is indeed a real story. And it is a colonial story. It hit the headlines in March 1967, when international newspapers and magazines such as *Life, Paris-Match,* and *Stern* started reporting the case of a curiously white gorilla cub, found in Equatorial Guinea and soon transported to Spain. *National Geographic,* which featured him on the cover in 1967 and 1970, reports the facts in detail. In the first of his two articles, Dr. Arthur J. Riopelle, a primatologist from Louisiana, triumphally described the humanization path of "Snowflake" with expressions such as "Jungle Ape Adopts Civilized Ways," relating the initial slowness in "taming" an (evidently traumatized) cub, that "allowed himself to be touched on the head, ears, arms, legs, and back" only after sixteen days, which is also when he was first "permitted to leave his cage." In the second article, however, Riopelle went so far as to describe the gorilla's comfort around people ("his public"), implying that the roles were reversed: "Time and again I have seen him stand erect to look at us through the window glass of his cage ... Are *we* on display?" That nonchalant "*we*" and the cruelly ironic game suggesting an impossible place swap confirm the abyssal divide separating Copito, caught in his singularity, and "his public."[77]

But how did this little gorilla become a celebrity? Here the personal story also reveals its bitter colonial flipside. In 1966, in Equatorial Guinea, a Fang tribe farmer named Benito Mañé killed a pack of gorillas, that – he claimed – were attacking his banana orchard. Clinging to the female's dead body, he spotted a curiously white cub. Aware of the exceptional discovery – and even more so of its monetary value – Mañé spared the baby gorilla and promptly sold him to Jordi Sabater Pi, a Catalan primatologist who took him to Spain. Before ending up in Barcelona's zoo in 1967, Copito de Nieve lived for some time with the family of the zoo's veterinarian, Román Luera Carbó, looked after by his wife and playing with their eight-year-old son Francisco and their basset hound Pompeia. A photo-reportage in *Life* shows, with captions in sheer Disney rhetoric, the "natural" integration of Copito within the fabric of his human "family."[78] During these months, he was strongly humanized – with toys, "boyish roughhousing" with his human "brother," "human" food, and shoes. After this forced anthropomorphic infancy, even filled with large display of affection, he was transferred to the zoo. There, he became not only a major attraction, but also the bearer of a genetic pool which had to be preserved at all costs. As Calvino also wrote in his *Repubblica* article, many ways were tried to have him generate white cubs, including mating with his own daughters. At the

---

[77] Quotes in Riopelle 1967: 446–448; and 1970: 492 (emphasis in the original).
[78] "Unique in All Gorilladom" 1967.

end of his life, Copito de Nieve had fathered twenty-two offspring by three different mates. Only six children survived to adulthood. However, they – and their children and grandchildren – were all black.[79]

As we read on the English Wikipedia page about him (which does not quote a source for this information), the Barcelona Zoo "had a protocol in place to have Snowflake's testicles harvested, upon his death, and placed in the frozen zoo as to reserve the option of having more offspring from him in the future." (Incidentally, the reductionism of this operation is quite remarkable: the ultimate dematerialization of the gorilla's semiotic world is in fact symbolically concentrated in the collection of his genes, as if they were significant per se, independently from his natural habitat.) Finally, in 2003, Copito fell ill with skin cancer and was euthanized. In Spain he was literally a superstar, inspiring books and films. After his death, an asteroid was named after him.[80]

The thing that strikes one most, when reading the reports about Copito – and those from the *National Geographic* magazine are no exception – is the candor with which his humanization and entry into the zoo are presented, almost as if they were the ineluctable destiny of such a unique "specimen." As many primatologists have pointed out, humanizing practices often increase the previous trauma experienced by formerly wild apes – the trauma of capture, loss of parents and siblings, and detachment from the original *Umwelt* – by adding to it the trauma of forcefully leaving their adoptive family once their physical strength becomes a threat to people. "They're stuck between two worlds," Jane Goodall commented on chimpanzees caught in a similar situation: "They've never learned to be a chimpanzee and they can never become a human" (Yuhas 2015). And this is often a mutual trauma even for the little humans of the family, as Karen Joy Fowler's stirring book *We Are All Completely Beside Ourselves* (2013) highlights in a lyrical and powerfully evocative way. In this novel, a mysteriously lost sister becomes the cipher of the life of a woman, Rosemary, who finally finds her as a chimpanzee in a zoo cage: "I didn't know what she was thinking or feeling. Her body had become unfamiliar to me. And yet, at the very same time, I recognized everything about her. My sister, Fern. . . . As if I were looking in a mirror" (2013: 308). As Louise Westling noted in her examination of the "dangerous intersubjectivities"

---

[79] To examine this "fixation" with the gorilla's whiteness from the point of view of race theory and coloniality at large would disclose further significant aspects of this story. Not coincidentally, Copito is the *white* animal that comes from a *black* country that was a Spanish colony until 1968. I thank Oswaldo Estrada and Priscilla Layne for this insightful observation.

[80] These pieces of information are taken from https://en.wikipedia.org/wiki/Snowflake_(gorilla) (last accessed: December 14, 2020). I have found useful information on Copito de Nieve in the pages that Wikipedia's sites in Italian, Spanish, and English dedicate to him. See also Oppes 2003.

between humans and other primates, "Rosemary confesses both her incomprehension and her profound identification, trapped in a middle space between species and robbed of what had seemed a full sibling relationship in their very young childhood" (2016: 33). Although not a lost "family member" for Mr. Palomar, Copito de Nieve is also a mysterious mirror that reveals the hubris of creating cultural gulfs between evolutionary kin that are prevented from recognizing each other as brotherly subjects.

The colonial side of Copito's story – a story, where the animal is, materially and by definition, disempowered and "othered" – is not limited to his case, though. In fact, it prompts a further and more general consideration. Modern zoos, indeed, are historically colonial institutions. As Randy Malamud explained in his monumental *Reading Zoos* (1998), the zoo is an expression of imperialist capitalism and of its systematic attempt to commodify the living world by transforming all conquered subjects into subaltern beings. The biopolitical dimension of this phenomenon is evident in the fact that these collections of exotic animals, which along with their habitat have suffered the onslaught of colonial predators, speak of a power that is at the same time material and cultural: the power to rewrite the natural world in terms of authoritarian master narratives and more reassuring representations, imposing alien cultural models upon it.

By and large, the possession of captive animals has always been a distinctive trait of political grandeur: "Potentates demonstrate their power by appearing to sustain a cosmos," writes Yi-Fu Tuan in his history of animal domestication (1984: 75). Modern zoos are preceded by a long record of animal collecting that dates back to the empires of Assyria and Babylonia and includes Egyptian as well as Chinese dynasties. The first testimony of a park where "a large number of beasts were kept for the exclusive contemplation and enjoyment of the monarch," comes from China, dated around 1150 BC (Tuan 1984: 21). Prepared by the thriving of the geopolitical structures of mercantilism of the Renaissance, which made it possible to further develop the practice of trading and collecting animals, zoos became public institutions in the first decades of the nineteenth century and in the Victorian age, coinciding with the industrial revolution – one of the possible triggering moments of the Anthropocene. One of the first of its kind, the London Zoological Society, for example, was founded in 1826 by Sir Stamford Raffles with the purpose of collecting the animals he had captured in Southeastern Asia while working as a trader for the East India Company. "He plundered exotic commercial goods in his professional employment, and plundered the animal world as a hobby," writes Malamud, who adds: "The zoos and the animals thus became part of the discourse that reinforced the hegemonies of imperialism" (2018: 402). An integral part of this discourse is the fact that, in the late nineteenth century, the animals displayed in the zoo cages of all the great European and American cities, were, in some cases, also human animals. As Oliver Hochadel writes in "Darwin in the Monkey Cage," "Humans staged as strange and exotic were exhibited alongside lions and monkeys" (2010: 99). Based on the often-racist biases of the zoology and anthropology of the time, this "zoo Darwinism" reinforced the hegemonic narrative according to which Africans and Asians were closer to animals than were Europeans. Popular attractions included Eskimos exhibited along with their sled dogs, Sudanese people with their camels, and Sri Lankans with elephants. The most infamous – and tragic – case is that of the Congolese pygmy Ota Benga, who in 1906 was exhibited at the Bronx Zoo in the same cage as an orangutan. Following visitors' protests, he was released. He committed suicide in 1916, surrounded by a hostile environment and frustrated at not being able to return to the Congo – even in his case, a lost existential *Umwelt*.[81] With a simple linguistic connection, one cannot help noticing that in zoos, life is *zoe*, not *bios*: a "bare life" completely disentangled from its web of meanings and socioecological complexity, something to be put on display in its nakedness and completely left at the mercy of a sovereign power, as Giorgio Agamben (1998) would say. With his poetic rendering of Copito's captive existence as *zoe*, Calvino is implicitly claiming his right to be inscribed as a full-fledged citizen in the realm of *bios*, a social life teeming with meanings.[82]

Today, after so much debating and researching, we may say that zoos look less like concentration camps than they did a few years ago, and perhaps in some cases their action is crucial to preserve species that would otherwise face extinction.[83] However, it is equally crucial to note that in no form can the zoo – an expression of the imperialism that is at the roots of this era that many call "Capitalocene" – serve as an alibi for the damage that the Sixth Extinction inflicts on the living dynamics of our planet. Still, where it survives in its "classic" form, the zoo is "a cultural fossil" (Spotte 2006: 17). It is an institution that hardly allows us to recognize the Other as embodied in a kindred being, despite the fact that this Other has a face that, like the face of the albino gorilla, so closely resembles our own. This is the mark of the Anthropocene: the fact that the environment that creates new ecological proximities in the city is not

---

[81] An earlier and equally notorious example of "anthropological showcasing" (although not in specific connection to zoos) is the case of the South African Kohikohi woman Sarah Baartman (*c.*1775–1815). She was exhibited as a freak-show attraction in nineteenth-century Europe under the name "Hottentot Venus." After her premature death, she was displayed at Paris's Musée de l'Homme. Her body was only repatriated in 2002, upon Nelson Mandela's request. The case is often cited for its scientific racism, sexism, and colonialism. See Crais and Scully 2009. I thank Florence Babb for drawing my attention to Baartman's case.

[82] I thank Townsend Middleton for this suggestion.   [83] See the essays in Acampora 2010.

always able to create an ecosystem, because it cuts all possible ties, including cognitive ones.[84] To be endangered here is not only the ecology of biological systems, but also the ecology of mind, mined by this forcefully schizophrenic relationship with an Other who belongs to our evolutionary family. Still, it is surprising that in (and perhaps despite) this very landscape of concrete and cages, crisscrossed by the dynamics of power, Mr. Palomar – like Marcovaldo before him – is able to cultivate what Roberto Marchesini calls "animal epiphanies." These epiphanies allow him to feel compassion for the animals we encage and for those we eat, and surprise and wonder for the animals whose sign-world he does not understand: birds, turtles, geckos, and a gorilla. In the nonbinary and yet mysterious vision that Calvino delivers to us, the living world lies and lives in these crossings, these hybrid compositions. The Anthropocene is all that, too.

These singular beings in particular are Calvino's response to a generalized faceless vision of nonhuman subjectivity. The rabbit, the hen, the gorilla all represent the world that lies before and beyond the constructed abstractedness of their bodily lives as expressed by words such as "livestock," "lab items," "zoo specimens." With these stories, these beings regain their faces, their uniqueness, situating themselves in the same moral territory of the human observer and inviting us to take "a sideways glance of a vast nonhuman world that has been denigrated by the concepts, institutions, and practices associated with 'the human.'"[85]

Calvino's animals do have a face, a face that coincides with their own bodies, and that, also thanks to his fictional artifice, we can picture as surprised, perplexed, depressed, or desperate. As Charles Darwin has taught us, it is a face whose expressions, though different from ours, we are invited to recognize, more than ever now that the mechanisms and assemblages of our power over other species make these species "killable" as individuals, groups, or multitudes.[86]

At the end of "The Albino Gorilla," Calvino writes:

> Leaving the zoo, Mr. Palomar cannot dispel the image of the albino gorilla from his mind. ... At night, both during the hours of insomnia ... the great ape continues to appear to him. "Just as the gorilla has his tire, which serves as

---

[84] In a passage on zoos which has acquired the status of a classic of ecological discourse, Umberto Eco has observed: "Where does the truth of ecology lie?" ... Here we can speak more legitimately of an Industry of the Fake because we find a Disneyland for animals" (1983: 49). In another ecocritical classic, Dana Phillips's *The Truth of Ecology*, this passage is commented on as follows: "given its undeniably alive yet tame animals, its natural yet manmade habitats, the zoo seemed to acknowledge the truth of ecology and yet, in good hyperrealistic fashion, it also seemed to make this truth into a lie, by dislocating and distorting it" (2003: 21).

[85] Calarco 2011: 56.   [86] See Acampora 2012; Gruen 2012.

tangible support for a raving, wordless speech," he thinks, "so I have this image of a great white ape. We all turn in our hands an old, empty tire through which we try to reach some final meaning, which words cannot achieve." (1985: 83)

This image that Calvino/Mr. Palomar carries with him, out of the zoo, now is ours, too. By passing it on to us, Calvino forces us to think about the singular losses – infinite extinctions taking place in the cages of the world's zoos. They are joint extinctions of habitats, individuals, and evolutionary plots, but they are also extinctions of communities of signs, of languages, of kin.

7 Epilogue

Life on the planet in the time of the Anthropocene has many problematic faces, all of which are intertwined with our activities. The coronavirus pandemic has violently shown how these activities interfere with the dynamics of biological systems, giving rise to unpredictable and uncontrollable effects. Teeming with nonhuman life, Calvino's works channel a precise message: we are not the only inhabitants of this planet, and we are not the protagonists of its imagination. Plants, insects, mammals, bacteria, shells, reptiles are all segments of a material imagination that grows, expands, and flourishes, around and within us. Words are also part of this sphere, which is both alive and cognitive. Calvino knew it very well. He was literally a bio-logist, one who gives word to life, although he did so differently from his parents and his other scientist relatives. But he was the black sheep of the family. He was a writer.[87]

Among Calvino's animal tales are some that allow us to understand the dynamics of the Anthropocene: invasion of alien species, the exploitation and suppression of millions of individuals, habitat destruction, lost environments of signs and beings. Extinction, usually at the top of the list of the deepest wounds that affect the biosphere today, appears in his writings in indirect or metaphorical ways. He talks about it in an episode of *Cosmicomics*, where the protagonist Qfwfq plays the role of the last dinosaur left on earth. More existential than ironic, "The Dinosaurs" is perhaps one of his few animal stories in which the focus is entirely on the human. This, in particular, is a moral apologue on the image we have of the "other," a being that is difficult to recognize and yet impossible to keep out of our conversations, our ambivalent feelings, and our biology. In another short story, "The Petrol Pump" (1974), extinction is more radical, and we humans are the real dinosaurs: "The day the earth's crust reabsorbs the cities, this plankton sediment that was humankind will be covered by geological layers of asphalt and cement until in millions of years' time it

---

[87] So Calvino defines himself vis-à-vis his parents and relatives. In Accrocca 1960: 110–11.

thickens into oily deposits, on whose behalf we do not know" (1995, 175). Written during the early 1970s oil crisis and read today, this story speaks directly to the Anthropocene, reminding us that one of the legacies of our current ecological predicaments may be the reduction of the *Anthropos* to future fossils.

But the truth is that extinction has many forms, and Calvino realized this as early as 1951, when his father died. What he understood is that living beings are not the only ones that can become extinct. Even languages, words, names can slowly mutate, until they finally get lost. This is what he tells us in *The Road to San Giovanni* (*La strada di San Giovanni*), an autobiographical narrative written precisely to deal with his father's spiritual legacy. A professor of agronomy and experimental farmer, Mario Calvino had a daily habit. Every morning at dawn, in the company of his dog, he went to his estate, just outside Villa Meridiana. In the summer, one of his sons, briskly snatched from sleep, was forcefully "invited" to follow him. Mario's agricultural knowledge was not just one of methods or practices. It was also a knowledge of the names, terms, and language – scientific as well as vernacular – that botanists and growers master. So Italo remembers this language:

> The only things he saw in the world were plants and whatever had to do with plants, and he would say all their names out loud, in the absurd Latin botanists use, . . . and their popular names, too . . . in Spanish or in English or in our local dialect, and into this naming of plants he would put all his passion for exploring a universe without end, for venturing time and again to the furthest frontiers of a vegetable genealogy, opening up from every branch or leaf or nervation as it were a waterway for himself, within the sap, within the network that covers the green earth. (1993: 7)

Lost in this network, Italo instead admits: "I could recognize not a single plant or bird. The world of things was mute for me" (11–12). Inventing words that sounded similar to those used by his father in his botanical idiom, in the pages of *The Road* he honored – not without an enduring feeling of guilt – all that he had lost of this language, due to rebellion, lack of interest, or simply an excess of youth: a youth that soon would become a partisan struggle, harbinger of other extinctions and of other biological, linguistic, and political hybridizations.

But what if things were different? What if literature was a way to stem this extinction, and to help us recognize the eloquence of these apparently mute things? We find the answer in a 1949 story, "Adam, one afternoon." In a big house surrounded by a botanical garden, a boy and a girl meet, and begin a game made up of names and words that are embodied in the things themselves. It is a creative and joyful exercise in philosophical realism, in which frogs, scarabs, goldfish, Argentine ants suddenly appear together with their names, as gifts from an adolescent Adam to a girl whose mind is full of astonishment. *Nomina sunt res*. Adam is Libereso Guglielmi, an apprentice at Villa Meridiana and protégé of Mario, a fifteen-year-old anarchist bearing a name that in Esperanto means "freedom" and who will later become famous for his talent as a gardener. As always, Calvino lets things do the talking. Throwing himself, already in his twenties, outside the borders of the self and into the world, he is saying this: only as long as we are able to tell living stories about animals, plants, insects, and everything that today is threatened by the intrusiveness of a faceless *Anthropos* can we hope to persist within the endless universe of mineral, animal, and vegetable genealogies, within the sap, within the network that covers the green earth.

Bibliography

Abram, D. (2010). *Becoming Animal: An Earthly Cosmology*. New York: Pantheon.

Acampora, R. (2006). *Corporal Compassion: Animal Ethics and Philosophy of Body*. Pittsburgh: University of Pittsburgh Press.

Acampora, R., ed. (2010). *Metamorphoses of the Zoo: Animal Encounter after Noah*. Lanham: Lexington Books.

Acampora, R. (2012). Toward a Properly Post-Humanist Ethos of Somatic Sympathy. In G. R. Smulewicz-Zucker, ed. *Strangers to Nature: Animal Lives and Human Ethics*. Lanham: Lexington Books, pp. 235–248.

Accrocca, E. F., ed. (1960), *Ritratti su misura*. Venice: Sodalizio del libro.

Adams, C. (2018). *Neither Man nor Beast: Feminism and the Defense of Animals*. London: Bloomsbury.

Agamben, G. (1998). *Homo Sacer: Sovereign Power and Bare Life*. Trans. D. Heller-Roazen. Stanford: Stanford University Press.

Akhtar, A. (2018). Suffering for Science and How Science Supports the End of Anima Experiments. In A. Linzey and C. Linzey, eds., *Palgrave Handbook of Practical Animal Ethics*. London: Palgrave Macmillan, pp. 475–492.

Alaimo, S. (2015). Animal. In J. Adamson, W. Gleason, and D. Pellow, eds. *Keywords for Environmental Studies*. New York: New York University Press, pp. 9–13.

Amberson, D. and Past, E. M., eds. (2014). *Thinking Italian Animals: Animals and the Posthuman in Italian Literature and Film*. New York: Palgrave Macmillan.

Armiero, M. (2021). *Wasteocene: Stories from the Global Dump*. Cambridge: Cambridge University Press.

Belpoliti, M. (2006). *L'occhio di Calvino*. Turin: Einaudi.

Berger, J. (1980). *About Looking*. New York: Vintage.

Bolongaro, E. (2009). Calvino's Encounter with the Animal: Anthropomorphism, Cognition and Ethics in *Palomar. Quaderni d'italianistica*, 30(2): 105–128.

Brambell, F. W. R. (1965). *Report of the Technical Committee to Enquire into the Welfare of Animals Kept under Intensive Livestock Husbandry Systems*. London: Her Majesty's Stationery Office.

Bubandt, N. and Tsing, A. (2018). Feral Dynamics of Post-Industrial Ruin: An Introduction. *Journal of Ethnobiology*, 38(1): 1–7.

Calarco, M. (2011). Identity, Difference, Indistinction. *The New Centennial Review*, 11: 41–60.

Calvino, I. (1958). *I racconti*. Turin: Einaudi.

Calvino, I. (1971). *The Watcher & Other Stories*. Transl. W. Weaver. New York: Harcourt Brace Jovanovich.

Calvino, I. (1980). Visita a un gorilla albino. *La Repubblica*, May 16.

Calvino, I. (1983a). *Difficult Loves. Smog. A Plunge into Real Estate*. Trans. W. Weaver. London: Picador.

Calvino, I. (1983b). *Marcovaldo, or The Seasons in the City*. Trans. W. Weaver. San Diego: Harcourt Brace Jovanovich.

Calvino, I. (1985). *Mr. Palomar*. Trans. W. Weaver. San Diego: Harcourt Brace Jovanovich.

Calvino, I. (1993). *The Road to San Giovanni*. Trans. T. Parks. New York: Pantheon.

Calvino, I. (2000). *Lettere 1940–1985*. L. Baranelli, ed. Milan: Mondadori.

Calvino, I. (2001). *Saggi 1945–1985*. 2 vols. M. Barenghi, ed. Milan: Mondadori.

Calvino, I. (1995). *Numbers in the Dark and Other Stories*. Trans. T. Parks. New York: Penguin.

Calvino, I. (2003). *Romanzi e racconti*. 3 vols. C. Milanini, ed. Milan: Mondadori.

Calvino, I. (2012). *Sono nato in America... Interviste 1951–1985*. L. Baranelli, ed. Milan: Mondadori.

Calvino, I. (2013). *Letters, 1941–1985*. Selected and with an introduction by M. Wood. Trans. M. McLaughlin. Princeton: Princeton University Press.

Carnemolla, C. (2019). Animali-umani e non- nel Capitalocene: *La gallina di reparto* di Calvino. *Scienza e Filosofia*, 21: 164–178.

Carson, R. (1962). *Silent Spring*. Boston: Houghton Mifflin.

Castello, G. (n.d.) Storia di un'invasione: la formica dell'Argentina. Bollettino Insetti. www.uomoinerba.it/formiche.htm

CeRSAA (Centro di Sperimentazione e Assistenza Agricola) (undated). *Life Sumflower. Pieghevole Nitrati*. www.cersaa.it/wp-content/uploads/2015/06/Nitrati.pdf

Chigi, A. (1968). *Trattato di avicoltura*. Turin: UTET.

Choe, D. H., Villafuerte, D. B., and Tsutsui, N. D. (2012). Trail Pheromone of the Argentine Ant, Linepithema humile (Mayr) (Hymenoptera: Formicidae). *PloS one*, 7(9): e45016. https://doi.org/10.1371/journal.pone.0045016

Crais, C. C. and Scully, P. (2009). *Sara Baartman and the Hottentot Venus: A Ghost Story and a Biography*. Princeton: Princeton University Press.

Crutzen, P. J. and Stoermer, E. F. (2000). The "Anthropocene." *Global Change Newsletter*, 41: 17.

Dawson, A. (2016). *Extinction: A Radical History*. New York: OR Books

Dawson, A. (2017). *Extreme Cities: The Peril and Promise of Urban Life in the Age of Climate Change*. New York: Verso.

de Waal, F. (2006). *Our Inner Ape: A Leading Primatologist Explains Why We Are Who We Are*. New York: Riverhead.

de Waal, F. (2019). *Mama's Last Hug: Animal Emotions and What They Tell Us about Ourselves*. New York: W. W. Norton.

Delort R. (1984). *Les animaux ont une histoire*. Paris: Seuil.

Despret, V. (2016). *What Would Animals Say If We Asked the Right Questions*. Trans. B. Buchanan. Minneapolis: University of Minnesota Press.

Despret, V. (2017). Afterword: It Is an Entire World That Has Disappeared. In D. B. Rose, T. van Dooren, and M. Chrulew, eds. *Extinction Studies: Stories of Time, Death, and Generations*. New York: Columbia University Press, pp. 217–222.

Driscoll C. A., Menotti-Raymond, M., Roca, A. L., et al. (2007). The Near Eastern Origin of Cat Domestication. *Science*, 317(5837): 519–523.

Eco, U. (1983). *Travels in Hyperreality*. Trans. W. Weaver. New York: Harcourt Brace Jovanovich.

Erickson W. P., Johnson, G. D, and Young Jr., D. P. (2005). A Summary and Comparison of Bird Mortality from Anthropogenic Causes with an Emphasis on Collisions. *USDA Forest Service Gen. Tech. Rep.* PSW-GTR-191. www .fs.fed.us/psw/publications/documents/psw_gtr191/psw_gtr191_1029-1042_erickson.pdf

Farm Animal Welfare Council/Farm Animal Welfare Committee (n.d.). Five Freedoms. https://webarchive.nationalarchives.gov.uk/20121010012427/http://www.fawc.org.uk/freedoms.htm

Farmer, J. (2017). Technofossils. In G. Mitman, M. Armiero, and R. S. Emmett, eds. *Future Remains: A Cabinet of Curiosities for the Anthropocene*. Chicago: University of Chicago Press, pp. 191–199.

Ferretti, G. C. (1989). *Le capre di Bikini: Calvino giornalista e saggista 1945–1985*. Rome: Editori Riuniti.

Ferrua, P. (1977). Il sostrato sanremese nella narrativa di Italo Calvino. *Italica*, 54(3): 367–380.

Foucault, M. (1997). Of Other Spaces: Utopias and Heterotopias [1967]. In Neil Leach, ed. *Rethinking Architecture: A Reader in Cultural Theory*. New York: Routledge, pp. 350–356.

Fowler, K. J. (2013). *We Are All Completely Beside Ourselves*. New York: G. P. Putnam's Sons.

Francione G. (2000). *Introduction to Animal Rights: Your Child or the Dog?* Philadelphia: Temple University Press.

Gan, E., Tsing, A. L., Swanson, H., and Bubandt, N. (2017). Introduction: Haunted Landscapes of the Anthropocene. In A. L. Tsing, H. Swanson,

E. Gan, and N. Bubandt, eds. *Arts of Living on a Damaged Planet: Ghosts and Monsters of the Anthropocene*. Minneapolis: University of Minnesota Press, pp. G1–G14.

Garrard, G. (2014). Ferality Tales. In G. Garrard, ed. *The Oxford Handbook of Ecocriticism*. Oxford: Oxford University Press, pp. 241–259.

Giraud, T., Pedersen, J. S., and Keller, L. (2002). Evolution of Supercolonies: The Argentine Ants of Southern Europe. *Proceedings of the National Academy of Sciences of the United States of America*, 99(9): 6075–6079. https://doi.org/10.1073/pnas.092694199

Gramsci, A. (1977). *Selections from the Prison Notebooks*. Trans. and ed. by Q. Hoare and G. N. Smith. New York: International Publishers

Grimm, C. L. W., Thayer, J. H., and Wilke, C. G. (1887). *A Greek-English Lexicon of the New Testament*. New York: Harper and Brothers.

Gruen, L. 2012. Navigating Difference (Again): Animal Ethics and Entangled Empathy. In G. R. Smulewicz-Zucker, ed. *Strangers to Nature: Animal Lives and Human Ethics*. Lanham: Lexington Books, pp. 213–234.

Gruen, L. (2015). *Entangled Empathy: An Alternative Ethic for Our Relationships with Animals*. Brooklyn, NY: Lantern Books

Haraway, D. (2008). *When Species Meet*. Minneapolis: Minnesota University Press.

Haraway, D. (2016). *Staying with the Trouble: Making Kin in the Chthulucene*. Minneapolis: Minnesota University Press.

Hochadel, O. (2010). Darwin in the Monkey Cage: The Zoological Garden as a Medium of Evolutionary Theory. In D. Brantz, ed. *Beastly Natures: Animals, Humans, and the Study of History*. Charlottesville: University of Virginia Press, pp. 81–107.

Hu, Y., S. Hu, W. Wang, et al. (2014). Earliest Evidence of Commensal Cats. *Proceedings of the National Academy of Sciences*, 111(1) 116–120.

Inglis-Arkell, E. (2015). These Ants Took Over The World, And We Just Noticed. *Gizmodo*, June 22. Online. https://io9.gizmodo.com/these-ants-took-over-the-world-and-we-just-noticed-1712998011

Iovino, S. (2018). Italo Calvino and the Landscapes of the Anthropocene: A Narrative Stratigraphy. In S. Iovino, E. Cesaretti, and E. Past, eds. *Italy and the Environmental Humanities: Landscapes, Natures, Ecologies*. Charlottesville: University of Virginia Press, pp. 67–77.

Irvine L. (2017). Animal Sheltering. In L. Kalof, ed. *The Oxford Handbook of Animal Studies*. Oxford: Oxford University Press, pp. 98–115.

Johnson, S., ed. (2010). *Bioinvaders*. Cambridge: The White Horse Press.

Kirksey, E. S., ed. (2014). *The Multispecies Salon*. Durham, NC: Duke University Press.

Knight, A. (2011). *The Costs and Benefits of Animal Experiments*. New York: Palgrave Macmillan.

Kristensen, E., Penha-Lopes, G., Delefosse, M., et al. (2012). What Is Bioturbation? The Need for a Precise Definition for Fauna in Aquatic Sciences. *MEPS – Marine Ecology Progress Series* 446 (February 2): 285–302.

Lestel, D. (2002). The Biosemiotics and Phylogenesis of Culture. *Social Science Information* 41(1): 35–68.

Lestel, D. (2016). *Eat This Book: A Carnivore's Manifesto*. Transl. Gary Steiner. New York: Columbia University Press.

Lestel, D., Bussolini, J., and Chrulew, M. (2014). The Phenomenology of Animal Life. *Environmental Humanities*, 5: 125–148.

Linzey, A., and C. Linzey, eds. (2018). *Palgrave Handbook of Practical Animal Ethics*. London: Palgrave Macmillan.

Lowe S. J., M. Browne, and S. Boudjelas (2000). *100 of the World's Worst Invasive Alien Species*. IUCN/SSC Invasive Species Specialist Group (ISSG), Auckland, New Zealand. www.issg.org/pdf/publications/worst_100/english_100_worst.pdf.

Malamud, R. (1998). *Reading Zoos: Representations of Animals and Captivity*. New York: New York University Press.

Malamud, R. (2018). The Problem with Zoos. In Linda Kalof, ed. *The Oxford Handbook of Animal Studies*. New York: Oxford University Press, pp. 397–413.

Mann, Charles C. (2011 [1493]). *Uncovering the New World Columbus Created*. New York: Vintage.

Maran, T. (2015). Biosemiotics. In J. Adamson, W. Gleason, and D. Pellow, eds. *Keywords for Environmental Studies*. New York: New York University Press, pp. 29–31.

Maran, T. (2020). *Ecosemiotics: The Study of Signs in Changing Ecologies*. Cambridge: Cambridge University Press.

Marchesini, R. (2005). *Fondamenti di Zooantropologia*. Bologna: Alberto Perdisa.

Marchesini, R. (2017). *Over the Human: Post-humanism and the Concept of Animal Epiphany*. Transl. Sarah De Sanctis. Cham: Springer.

Margulis, L. (1998). *The Symbiotic Planet: A New Look at Evolution*. London: Phoenix.

Marino, Lori (2017). Thinking Chickens: A Review of Cognition, Emotion, and Behavior in the Domestic Chicken. *Animal Cognition* 20(2): 127–147.

Martinelli, D. (2010). *A Critical Companion to Zoosemiotics: People, Paths, Ideas*. Dordrecht: Springer.

Matiassi Cantarin, M. and Marino, M. C. (2018). Post-War Ecosophic Intuition: About the (Im)Possibility of Ecological Coexistence in *Marcovaldo, or The Seasons in the City* by Italo Calvino. *Humanities*, 7(64): 1–12.

Mattucci F., Oliveira, R., Lyons, L. A., Alves, P. C., and Randi, E. (2015). European Wildcat Populations Are Subdivided into Five Main Biogeographic Groups: Consequences of Pleistocene Climate Changes or Recent Anthropogenic Fragmentation? *Ecology and Evolution*, 6(1): 3–22.

Meysman, F., Middelburg, J. J., and Heip, C. H. (2006). Bioturbation: A Fresh Look at Darwin's Last Idea. *Trends in Ecology and Evolution*, 21(12): 688–695.

Mez, E. (1974). Calvino, Mario. In *Dizionario Biografico degli Italiani*. Vol. 17. Rome: Istituto dell'Enciclopedia Italiana Treccani. Online. www.treccani.it /enciclopedia/mario-calvino_%28Dizionario-Biografico%29/.

Miao, Y. W., Peng, M. S., Wu, G. S., et al. (2013). Chicken Domestication: An Updated Perspective Based on Mitochondrial Genomes. *Heredity*, 110: 277–282.

Monnerot, M., Vigne, J., Biju-Duval, C., et al. (1994). Rabbit and Man: Genetic and Historic Approach. *Genetics Selection Evolution*, 26, Suppl. 1: 167s-182s.

Moore, J., ed. (2015). *Capitalism in The Web of Life: Ecology and the Accumulation of Capital*. London: Verso.

Moore, J. (2016a) *Anthropocene or Capitalocene: Nature, History, and the Crisis of Capitalism*. Oakland: PM Press.

Moore J. (2016b). The Rise of Cheap Nature. In J. Moore, ed. *Anthropocene or Capitalocene*. Oakland: PM Press, pp. 68–115.

Morabito, A., ed. (2016). *VI Rapporto Nazionale Animali in Città*. Rome: Legambiente.

Noss R. F. and A. Y. Corripeders (1994). *Saving Nature's Legacy: Protecting and Restoring Biodiversity*. Washington, DC: Island Press.

Morton, T. (2011). Coexistence and Coexistents: Ecology without a World. In A. Goodbody and K. Rigby, eds. *Ecocritical Theory: New European Approaches*. Charlottesville: University of Virginia Press, pp. 168–180.

Morton, T. (2013). *Hyperobjects: Philosophy and Ecology after the End of the World*. Minneapolis: University of Minnesota Press.

Morton, T. (2016). *Dark Ecology: For a Logic of Future Coexistence*. New York : Columbia University Press.

National Chicken Council (n.d.). US Chicken Industry History. www .nationalchickencouncil.org/about-the-industry/history/

O'Connor, T. (2013). *Animals as Neighbors: The Past and Present of Commensal Species*. East Lansing: Michigan State University Press.

O'Connor, T. (2017). Commensal Species. In L. Kalof, ed. *The Oxford Handbook of Animal Studies*. New York: Oxford University Press, pp. 525–541.

Oppermann, S. (2018). The Scale of the Anthropocene: Material Ecocritical Reflections. *Mosaic*, 51(3): 1–17.

Oppes, A. (2003). Il lungo addio a 'Fiocco di neve': Barcellona piange il gorilla bianco. *La Repubblica*. September 30. Online: www.repubblica.it/2003/i/sezioni/esteri/fiocco/fiocco/fiocco.html.

Ottieri, O. (2001). *La linea gotica: Taccuino 1948–1958*. Parma: Guanda.

Ottoni C., Van Neer, W., De Cupere, B., et al. (2016). Anthropology, Genetics Of Cats and Men: The Paleogenetic History of the Dispersal of Cats in the Ancient World, bioRxiv 080028; https://doi.org/10.1101/080028

Owens, M. and J. Wolch (2017). Lively Cities: People, Animals, and Urban Ecosystems In L. Kalof, eds. *The Oxford Handbook of Animal Studies*. Oxford/New York: Oxford University Press.

Pasolini, P. P. (2014). *The Selected Poetry of Pier Paolo Pasolini*. Ed. and transl. S. Sartarelli. Chicago: University of Chicago Press.

Past, E. (2019). *Italian Ecocinema Beyond the Human*. Bloomington: Indiana University Press.

Peggs, K. (2018). Animal Suffering Matters. In A. Linzey and C. Linzey, eds., *Palgrave Handbook of Practical Animal Ethics*. London: Palgrave Macmillan, pp. 373–393.

PETA. (n.d.). Facts and Statistics About Animal Testing. www.peta.org/issues/animals-used-for-experimentation/animals-used-experimentation-fact sheets/animal-experiments-overview/

Perrella, S. (2010). *Calvino*. Laterza: Rome-Bari.

Peters, J., Lebrasseur, O., Best. J., et al. (2015). Questioning New Answers Regarding Holocene Chicken Domestication in China. *Proceedings of the National Academy of Sciences, USA* 112: E2415.

Phillips, D. (2003). *The Truth of Ecology: Nature, Culture, and Literature in America*. Oxford: Oxford University Press.

Philo C. and C. Wilbert (2000). Animal Spaces, Beastly Places: An Introduction. In C. Philo and C. Wilbert, eds. *Animal Spaces, Beastly Places: New Geographies of Human-Animal Relations*. London: Routledge, pp. 1–35.

Porcher, J. (2011). *Vivre avec les animaux: Une Utopie pour le XXIe siècle*. Paris: La Découverte.

Quammen, D. (1996). *The Song of the Dodo: Island Biogeography in an Age of Extinctions*. New York: Scribner.

Regan, T. (1983). *The Case for Animal Rights*. Berkeley: University of California Press.

Rigby, K. (2020). Carnal Relations: Pathogens, Provender and Embodied Co-presence. *The New Normal? An Environmental Humanities Response. Bifrost Online*: https://bifrostonline.org/kate-rigby/

Riopelle, A. J., (1967). Snowflake: The World's First White Gorilla. *National Geographic* 131 (March): 442–448.

Riopelle, A. J., (1970). Growing Up With Snowflake. *National Geographic* 138 (October): 490–503.

Rohman, C. (2009). On Singularity and the Symbolic: The Threshold of the Human in Calvino's *Mr. Palomar. Criticism*, 51(1): 63–78.

Rose, D. B. (2013). In the Shadow of All This Death. In J. Johnston and F. Probyn-Rapsey, eds. *Animal Death.* . Sydney: Sydney University Press, pp. 1–20.

Rose, D. B. (2015). Ethnography. In J. Adamson, W. Gleason, and D. Pellow, eds. *Keywords for Environmental Studies*. New York: New York University Press, pp. 110–112.

Rose, D. van Dooren, B., T., and Chrulew, M. (2017). Introduction: Telling Extinction Stories. In D. B. Rose, T. van Dooren, and M. Chrulew, eds. *Extinction Studies: Stories of Time, Death, and Generations*. New York: Columbia University Press, pp. 1–17.

Ross, S. (2003). Calvino and Animals: The Multiple Functions of Marcovaldo's Poisonous Rabbit. *Spunti e Ricerche*, 18: 29–40.

Sanna, A. (2018). The Hybrid "Biocitizen" In Italo Calvino's *Marcovaldo, Or The Seasons In The City*. In P. Verdicchio, ed. *Ecocritical Approaches to Italian Culture and Literature*. Lanham: Lexington, pp. 31–42.

Scarpa, D. (1999). *Italo Calvino*. Milan: Bruno Mondadori.

Seger, M. (2015). *Landscapes in Between: Environmental Change in Modern Italian Literature and Film*. Toronto: Toronto University Press.

Seigworth G. J. and M. Gregg (2010). An Inventory of Shimmers. In G. J. Seigworth and M. Gregg, eds. *The Affect Theory Reader*. Durham, NC: Duke University Press, pp. 1–25.

Serpell, J. A. (1996). *In the Company of Animals: A Study of Human–Animal Relationships*. Cambridge: Cambridge University Press.

Serpell, J. A. (2014). The Domestication and History of the Cat. In D. C. Turner and P. Bateson, eds. *The Domestic Cat: The Biology of its Behaviour*. Cambridge: Cambridge University Press, pp. 83–100.

Settis, S. (2012), *Paesaggio costituzione cemento: La battaglia per l'ambiente contro il degrado civile*. Turin: Einaudi.

Shepard P. (1998a). *Coming Home to the Pleistocene*. Washington, DC: Island Press.

Shepard, P. (1998b). *The Tender Carnivore and the Sacred Game*. Athens, GA: University of Georgia Press.

Smulewicz-Zucker, Gregory R. ed. (2012): *Strangers to Nature: Animal Lives and Human Ethics*. Lanham: Lexington.

Spotte, S. (2006). *Zoos in Postmodernism: Signs and Simulation*. Madison, NJ: Farleigh Dickinson University Press.

Steiner, G. (2016). Translator's Preface. In D. Lestel, *Eat This Book: A Carnivore's Manifesto*. New York: Columbia University Press, pp. ix–xv.

Swanson, H., A. Tsing, N. Bubandt, and E. Gan. (2017). Introduction: Bodies Tumbled into Bodies. In A. Tsing, H. Swanson, E. Gan, and N. Bubandt, eds. *Arts of Living on a Damaged Planet: Ghosts of the Anthropocene*. Minneapolis: University of Minnesota Press. M1-14.

Tallacchini, M. (2015). Gli animali nella "società europea della conoscenza": Contraddizioni e prospettive. *Animal Studies: Rivista italiana di antispecismo*, 12: 9–30.

Thomas, K. (1983). *Man and the Natural World: Changing Attitudes in England 1500–1800*. New York: Penguin.

Tixier-Boichard, M., B. Bed'hom, and X. Rognon (2011). Chicken Domestication: From Archeology to Genomics. *Comptes Rendus Biologies*, 334: 197–204.

Todd, N. B. (1978). An Ecological, Behavioural Genetic Model for the Domestication of the Cat. *Carnivore* 1: 52–60.

Trevisani G. (1924). *Pollicoltura*. Milan: Hoepli.

Trevisani, G. (1902). Sull'importanza dell'Avicoltura in Italia come fattore di benessere economico, *Atti Società Agraria di Bologna*, January 12.

Tsing, A. L. (2015). *The Mushroom at the End of the World: On the Possibility of Life in Capitalist Ruins*. Princeton: Princeton University Press.

Tsing, A. L., H. Swanson, E. Gan, and N. Bubandt, eds. (2017). *Arts of Living on a Damaged Planet*. Minneapolis: University of Minnesota Press.

Tuan, Yi-Fu. (1984). *Dominance and Affection: The Making of Pets*. New Haven, CT: Yale University Press.

Turri, E. (2014 [1990]). *Semiologia del paesaggio italiano*. Venice: Marsilio.

Uexküll, J. von (2010). *A Foray into the Worlds of Animals and Humans: With a Theory of Meaning*. Transl. J. O'Neil. Introduction by D. Sagan. Afterword by G. Winthorp-Young. Minneapolis: Minnesota University Press.

Unspecified author (1967). Unique in All Gorilladom: Román Luera Carbó's Snowflake, *Life* 62, March 31: 69–70.

Vallerani, F. (2013). *Italia desnuda: Percorsi di resistenza nel paese del cemento*. Milan: Unicopli.

Van Wilgenburg, E., C. W.Torres, and N. D. Tsutsui (2010). The Global Expansion of A Single Ant Supercolony. *Evolutionary Applications*, 3(2): 136–143.

Wang, M. S., Thakur, M., Peng, MS., et al. (2020). 863 Genomes Reveal the Origin and Domestication of Chicken. *Cell Research* 30: 693–701.

Weis, T. (2013). *The Ecological Hoofprint: The Global Burden of Industrial Livestock.* London: Zed Books.

Westling, L. (2013). *The Logos of the Living World: Merleau-Ponty, Animals, and Language.* New York: Fordham University Press.

Westling, L. (2016). Dangerous Intersubjectivities from Dionysos to Kanzi. In M. Tønnessen, K. Armstrong Oma, and S. Rattasepp, eds. *Thinking about Animals in the Age of the Anthropocene.* Lanham: Lexington Books, pp. 209–231.

Wilkie, R. (2017). Animals as Sentient Commodities. In L. Kalof, ed. *The Oxford Handbook of Animal Studies.* Oxford: Oxford University Press, pp. 279–301.

Williams, M., J. Zalasiewicz, P. Haff, C. Schwägerl, A. D. Barnosky, and E. C. Ellis. (2015). The Anthropocene Biosphere. *The Anthropocene Review* 2(3): : 196–219.

Wolch, J. (1998). Zoöpolis. In J. Wolch and J. Emel, eds. *Animal Geographies,* London: Verso, pp. 119–137.

Wolfe, C. (2017). Foreword. In D. B. Rose, T. van Dooren, and M. Chrulew, eds. *Extinction Studies.* New York: Columbia University Press, pp. vii–xvi.

Yuhas, A. (2015). Jane Goodall Hails "Awakening" as US Labels All Chimpanzees Endangered. *The Guardian*, June 12, 2015. Online. www.theguardian.com/world/2015/jun/12/jane-goodall-us-chimpanzees-endangered

Zalasiewicz, J. (2016). The Extraordinary Strata of the Anthropocene. In S. Oppermann and S. Iovino, eds., *Environmental Humanities: Voices from the Anthropocene.* Lanham: Rowman & Littlefield, pp. 115–131.

Zalasiewicz, J., C. N. Waters, and M. Williams. (2014). Human Bioturbation, and the Subterranean Landscape of the Anthropocene. *Anthropocene* 6: 3–9.

Acknowledgments

I would like to express my appreciation to Domenico Scarpa, Louise Westling, Timo Maran, Elena Past, and Maurizio Valsania for their invaluable suggestions on all the topics and aspects of this research. John Tallmadge and the two anonymous reviewers provided amazing editorial feedback, which helped my manuscript in its final stages.

Italo Calvino's Animals is part of a larger research on Calvino and ecology started at the Rachel Carson Center for Environment and Society, Munich. My gratitude goes to Christof Mauch and all the fellows of the 2017–18 cohort: their friendship keeps me going.

This Element was drafted during a semester-long research leave supported by the University of North Carolina's Institute of Arts and Humanities. This list of acknowledgments would, therefore, be incomplete without the names of Tim Marr and Philip Hollingsworth, respectively Director of the Faculty Fellows Program and Program Administrator; and of the 2021 Spring Faculty Fellows: Florence Babb, Maya Berry, Oswaldo Estrada, Priscilla Layne, Townsend Middleton, Courtney Rivard, Katherine Turk, and Claudia Yaghoobi. One of the most stimulating experiences of the bewildering Covid-19 season, the intellectual joyfulness and productivity of these "remote" interdisciplinary conversations breathes in these pages and in my memory.

Cambridge Elements ☰

Environmental Humanities

Louise Westling
University of Oregon

Louise Westling is an American scholar of literature and environmental humanities who was a founding member of the Association for the Study of Literature and Environment and its President in 1998. She has been active in the international movement for environmental cultural studies, teaching and writing on landscape imagery in literature, critical animal studies, biosemiotics, phenomenology, and deep history.

Serenella Iovino
University of North Carolina at Chapel Hill

Serenella Iovino is Professor of Italian Studies and Environmental Humanities at the University of North Carolina at Chapel Hill. She has written on a wide range of topics, including environmental ethics and ecocritical theory, bioregionalism and landscape studies, ecofeminism and posthumanism, comparative literature, eco-art, and the Anthropocene.

Timo Maran
University of Tartu

Timo Maran is an Estonian semiotician and poet. Maran is Professor of Ecosemiotics and Environmental Humanities and Head of the Department of Semiotics at the University of Tartu. His research interests are semiotic relations of nature and culture, Estonian nature writing, zoosemiotics and species conservation, and semiotics of biological mimicry.

About the Series

The environmental humanities is a new transdisciplinary complex of approaches to the embeddedness of human life and culture in all the dynamics that characterize the life of the planet. These approaches reexamine our species' history in light of the intensifying awareness of drastic climate change and ongoing mass extinction. To engage this reality, Cambridge Elements in Environmental Humanities builds on the idea of a more hybrid and participatory mode of research and debate, connecting critical and creative fields.

Cambridge Elements ≡

Environmental Humanities

Elements in the Series

A full series listing is available at: www.cambridge.org/EIEH

Printed in the United States
by Baker & Taylor Publisher Services